MW00337529

COOK IT UP

Alex Guarnaschelli + Ava Clark

COOK IT UP

BOLD MOVES for FAMILY FOODS

CLARKSON POTTER/ PUBLISHERS
New York

Copyright © 2023 by
Alex Guarnaschelli
Copyright © 2023 by Ava Clark
Photographs Copyright © 2023
by Suech and Beck
Photographs Copyright © 2023
by Ken Goodman
All rights reserved.

Published in the United States by Clarkson Potter/Publishers, an imprint of Random House, a division of Penguin Random House LLC, New York.
ClarksonPotter.com
RandomHouseBooks.com

CLARKSON POTTER is a trademark and POTTER with colophon is a registered trademark of Penguin Random House LLC.

Library of Congress Cataloging-in-Publication Data
Names: Guarnaschelli, Alex, 1969– author. | Clark, Ava, author.
Title: Cook it up : bold moves for family foods / Alex Guarnaschelli + Ava Clark ; photographs by Suech and Beck.
Identifiers: LCCN 2022055731 (print) | LCCN 2022055732 (ebook) | ISBN 9780593577981 (hardcover) | ISBN 9780593577998 (ebook)
Subjects: LCSH: Cooking. | LCGFT: Cookbooks.

Classification: LCC TX714 .G795 2023 (print) | LCC TX714 (ebook) | DDC 641.5—dc23/eng/20221121
LC record available at https://lccn.loc.gov/2022055731
LC ebook record available at https://lccn.loc.gov/2022055732

ISBN: 978-0-593-57798-1
Ebook ISBN: 978-0-593-57799-8

Printed in China

Illustrations by Ava Clark

Cover photographs and photographs on pages 2, 4, 8, 9, 14, 32, 40, 43-45, 50, 51, 55, 57, 68, 71, 72, 74, 76, 86, 96, 99, 101, 105, 107, 112, 114, 118, 121, 127, 132, 138, 139, 142, 145, 149, 159, 162, 163, 167, 168, 170, 173, 177, 179, 182, 187, 191-193, 201, 203, 204, 208, 209, 211, 213, 216-219, 225, 226, 228, 232, 240.
Photographers: Suech and Beck
Food Stylist: Melanie Stuparyk
Food Stylist Assistant: Jonah Snitman
Prop Stylist: Maeve Sheridan

Photographs on pages 13, 20, 23, 24, 27, 28, 33, 34, 38, 39, 49, 52, 60, 64-66, 80, 81, 83, 87, 88, 92, 95, 102, 108, 113, 116, 124, 126, 129, 130, 134, 141, 146, 150, 154-156, 164, 174, 183, 184, 188, 197, 198, 223.
Photograher: Ken Goodman

Editor: Raquel Pelzel
Editorial Assistant: Bianca Cruz
Designer: Stephanie Huntwork
Production Editor: Terry Deal
Production Manager: Jessica Heim
Compositors: Merri Ann Morrell and Hannah Hunt
Copy Editor: Dolores York
Proofreaders: Rachel Markowitz and Sasha Tropp
Indexer: Elizabeth T. Parson
Marketer: Brianne Sperber
Publicists: David Hawk and Natalie Yera

10 9 8 7 6 5 4 3 2 1

First Edition

TO MY DAUGHTER, AVA, AND SWEET
LEON DUVAL LE CHIFFRE. OUR LITTLE
FAMILY IS EVERYTHING. FOOD IS OUR
LOVE AND FAMILY LANGUAGE—WE
HOPE YOU MAKE IT PART OF YOURS.

CONTENTS

BREAKFAST
ACCORDING TO AVA

LUNCH BOX

SANDWICHES, TARTINES + TACOS

SNACKS + HORS D'

PASTAS

INTRODUCTION

Ava's relationship to food fascinates me. I know she is my daughter, but she's actually somewhat of an enigma to me. Whereas I learned to cook in school and via the work-your-way-up-the-ranks classic French brigade system, Ava just cooks—always with curiosity and with so much confidence. I think the biggest (and most exciting) surprise for me as her mom has been watching her slowly turn into a home cook. As a chef who grew up in a house with two parents who constantly cooked, my relationship to food is loaded with meaning. I have food memories with my parents, decades of repetitive cooking in restaurants, and years of judging and cooking on television under my belt. I almost can't pick up an egg without considering twenty-five dishes I've tasted or the twelve ways I want to cook it. Ava comes to the table far less inhibited; she adds small touches that seem obvious and natural to her—things she didn't learn from me, by the way. TikTok, TV, and restaurants have been her cooking schools. For example, she'll go into the kitchen and cook up scrambled eggs, fry some capers on the side, then gently mix them in. She'll cook bacon for a BLT carefully, strip by strip, and then smear homemade herb butter on the toasted bread before sandwiching it together. By comparison, I didn't even know how to cook bacon when I was a young teenager.

Ava and I share a compulsion to cook—we love to do it—and it comes naturally to us. Cooking is in our DNA. And our followers on social media like to watch us cook together—and are always asking Ava (and asking me about Ava) what she's cooking and how she's cooking it. When we were approached about collaborating on a cookbook, she was sitting at the kitchen counter eating a burger with a small makeshift batch of jalapeño and roasted pepper jam on top. It smelled so good. "How did you make that, Ava?" I asked. She stared at me for a second and smiled. "I don't know, Mom. You're the Iron Chef around here. Aren't you supposed to be answering *my* questions about food?" Truth is, from a dragon fruit salad with a squeeze of lime and a drizzle of honey (page 42) to kimchi pancakes made from scratch (page 103), Ava represents the next generation of cooks who will explore the kitchen with great curiosity. On the contrary, I think I represent my family's history (experiences that are not limited to parents—cousins, family friends, stepparents, and neighbors also count in this equation).

Ava and I talked a lot about how this book should be. We tossed around the idea of how cool it would be to make it an ode to the fundamentals of cooking, so that any kid could get started developing their own repertoire of dishes in the kitchen. But the truth is that we just want kids and adults to cook together and share their ideas with one another. Ave told me, "I don't want kids to think they have to just cook kid food, Mom, okay?" We obviously encourage parents and friends to participate and help in the process. There are some recipes that even require or recommend a little adult assistance, and we call out those moments. (Adults can be good for moments where safety comes into play.) Ava has cooked with some of my friends, boyfriends, and other family members. Influences and support can come in many forms, and we always recommend it. Cooking is even more fun when done with and for the people you love.

You just need to start. Somewhere. And Ava and I both hope you begin here, with us. Let's cook—and better yet, let's eat.

Alex + Ava

GETTING STARTED
a manifesto for cooking with confidence

To us, cooking comes in two parts. Part one: shopping for food. We love supermarkets, greenmarkets, farm stands, and all types of specialty stores—and like most everyone else, we shop online, too. When we shop, it nurtures Ava's curiosity about flavors and ingredients. She will pick out condiments and spices along the way and experiment with them in her own dishes and cooking. It's interesting to watch kids explore personal taste and develop their own likes and dislikes. To that end, we feel it's important to share Ava's pantry (see page 15) as a starting point. The pantry provides some perspective on her ingredient choices and what she really enjoys using in her cooking—and specific brands she and I like most. Maybe some of you will end up trying some of these ingredients, too, and create a curated corner in your pantry.

Part two is the cooking itself. Some of the dishes in this book are simple; some require more technique. There is no judgment here. Feel free to use store-bought items to make a dish easier or more efficient to make. Some cooking is always better than no cooking at all! For example, buy pie dough at the grocery store and simply make the filling. Buy the cocktail sauce and only poach the shrimp. Buy a tart shell and only make the quiche filling. There are countless examples where buying ready-made elements for a recipe can be helpful—we encourage that. Working your way up from simple to more complex dishes is all part of the process of cooking (and it's why when you get to the more involved dishes, they truly don't seem so hard to make). The most important part is simple exploration. What is rewarding

when you make it, and what tastes delicious to you? We hope this book will help you enjoy answering those questions for yourself.

Sometimes Ava and I collaborate on a dish or a meal, and sometimes we cook simultaneously but separately. We let our kitchen breathe and give each other space. That said, we always cook with each other in mind. For example, Ava likes things spicy and can be particular about hot sauces. I like heat, too—but not as much as she does! So we cook knowing that some dishes can have a little bit of heat in them, but the spice level can always be adjusted or even eliminated. All the same, if we suggest a flavor that you don't like, simply remove the ingredient and carry on.

There is no blueprint or set of rules to follow when it comes to cooking—sure, there's a recipe, but it is more of a suggestion. You can and should improvise (with ingredients—not with technique). Also, try to embrace having failures in the kitchen. They're inevitable. Don't look at them as a reason to stop cooking—in fact, failures often make you a better cook because you learn along the way. You may make a mistake or over- or undercook things. It happens. Failing and learning is usually rewarding.

We are sharing a lot of our process, and maybe some of that will make its way into your home. Our hope is that ultimately, you will find dishes you enjoy making and invent ways to make them your own.

STIR BOILING PASTA SO IT DOESN'T STICK.

start with a
STOCKED PANTRY

Of course, Ava's pantry is my pantry, and my pantry is Ava's. I inherited a taste for many of the ingredients I use from my parents—they're items I'm used to from childhood. Ava, in turn, has created her own area in the pantry where her ingredients and flavors live. We get most of our pantry items from the grocery store, but there are some ingredients we do like to go to special places for—most of these ingredients are available online, too. Some of the ingredient sources we like: Kalustyan.com, Penzeys.com, and SOS-chefs.com for spices, vinegars, and condiments.

ALL-THE-TIME VEGETABLES

We need at least two heads of **garlic** on hand. This is a mandatory ingredient—in our house, garlic is often the base ingredient of all food. Sauces, soups, pastas, and other dishes are incomplete without garlic.

ONIONS are also a staple ingredient. They're so satisfying to chop and cook because the smell is out of this world. Onions are a superior vegetable because they're incredibly flexible, whether used in sauces, pickled, or diced for a soup or stew.

When to use which onion? The onion family can be confusing to navigate. There are no rules, really. Use what you like where you like it—this makes life easy—so if you don't have a yellow onion, sub in scallions or a red onion and vice versa. It's always, ultimately, about flavor. Generally speaking, use **red onions** for salsas, pickling, and sandwich toppings. **Yellow onions**, which are slightly sweeter and mellower than the red, go into soups, braises, stews, and sauces. A few **shallots** are great to have around, too. We use them in rice dishes, salads, and meat dishes. Quick-cooking and vibrant **scallions** are also great

to have for stir-fries, tuna and chicken salads, and even in quick-cooking soups served hot or cold.

SALTS, PEPPERS + SALTY ACCENTS

A kitchen without salt is like cornflakes without milk. You can really have a lot of fun with salt, and while there are so many to choose from, we really only cook with two types:

KOSHER SALT (Diamond Crystal brand is our absolute favorite) and **Maldon flaky sea salt**. Kosher salt is cheap and good for seasoning pretty much everything. Diamond Crystal is not too salty or dense, and forgives if you add a little too much. Maldon flaky sea salt provides that last kiss of seasoning before you dig in, so we refer to it as "the finishing salt." Its texture provides a cool crunch in addition to a salty touch.

A pepper mill filled to the brim with **black peppercorns** (we buy ours from Penzeys) is our favorite way to enlist pepper in a dish. To me, precracked black pepper tastes a little like sawdust. Cracking black pepper fresh is fun and makes food taste better. We grind it in the mill as we need it.

Beyond the classic black pepper, brined **green peppercorns** (La Caperelle) are a good item to have. Green peppercorns are by far our favorite type of peppercorn, mostly because they're not as overpowering as pink or black peppercorns, and they have that briny taste that is a great addition to sauces, especially for meats like pork chops or steak. Steak-like vegetables such as cauliflower, cabbage, and broccoli are tasty with a splash added, too.

Some people don't like **capers** (Jeff's Garden) because they're either too salty or too sweet, but a few capers in a sauce or salad can make the whole dish. Want to mellow the saltiness? Just soak them in plain cold water in the fridge for two to three days before using. Want to make them a crispy garnish? Drain the capers on a paper towel and then panfry in a little hot oil for a few minutes 'til crisped, then drain and sprinkle. Use the brine in the jar to season a salad dressing or a sauce.

THE SPICE RACK

DRIED OREGANO (Simply Organic) When you need oregano, dried oregano is the best option because it's mellower than fresh. It's excellent in a classic pizzeria spice mix with some garlic powder and red pepper flakes or in a dressing for a Greek salad. Dried oregano tastes very Mediterranean, making it a good choice for Italian-style dressings, chicken wings, and occasionally, pork chops.

GARLIC POWDER (Simply Organic) Besides coriander, garlic powder is a great seasoning for a spice rub for fish or meat. Next time you use fresh garlic in a recipe, try adding a dash of garlic powder to reinforce the fresh. It's a cool trick—like the garlic version of having back-up singers. It enhances the music (or, in this case, flavors).

GRANULATED GARLIC (McCormick) We have fresh garlic and garlic powder. Isn't that enough? Never. Granulated garlic is like little toasted pieces of garlic. It's chewy and almost has a browned garlic flavor. Honestly, we love it everywhere.

ONION POWDER (Simply Organic) Onion powder is mildly sweet but doesn't necessarily taste like onion. It also adds body and thickness to a sauce when you add a generous dash.

SWEET AND SMOKY PAPRIKA (Simply Organic) Sweet paprika or smoky, paprika (pimento) has less heat and spice when compared to cayenne but still offers a lot of taste. It also enriches the color of a sauce.

CORIANDER SEEDS (Penzeys) I think it's time everyone know that coriander seeds are the result of the flowering of cilantro plants, aka the most flavorful herb and spice there is. Toasted coriander seeds used in a sauce or spice rub are so tasty, almost floral (just shake them around in a skillet over medium heat until they smell fragrant). Coriander seeds added to pickling liquid (especially for pickling shallots) are absolutely amazing.

WHITE SESAME SEEDS
(Sushi Chef) Sesame seeds can be used whenever you want the richness of a nut but want to avoid using them. You can top almost any food with toasted sesame seeds—our favorite combos are sesame seeds sprinkled over steak, avocados, fresh or canned tuna, and bananas (trust us!).

BLACK SESAME SEEDS
(Sushi Chef) Black sesame seeds are a little different from white sesame seeds. They're less rich and almost earthier. They're excellent sprinkled over pickled cucumbers and also on tomatoes or the ramen noodles on page 63.

FURIKAKE (Nori Komi)
Furikake is basically three things: nori combined with toasted sesame seeds, and salt (and sometimes sugar, but that's not a good taste; check the label). Furikake is used as a topping, like on poke or over rice. Almost anything can be topped with furikake.

KOREAN CHILI FLAKES
(Tae-Kyung) Korean chili flakes are *very* different from your average chili flakes. They're great for kimchi, chili oil, and even stew. They're much spicier and have a more saturated red color than Italian dried red pepper flakes. If experimenting with spices and heat, you can sprinkle some on the kimchi pancakes on page 103.

VINEGARS + OILS

We always have **red wine vinegar** (Regina) and **apple cider vinegar** (Bragg) in the house. Acid balances heavy or creamy food—we use red wine vinegar *a lot*. It's great for pickling liquids, salad dressings, and even deglazing vegetables, especially oyster mushrooms, because it adds that acidic taste that is just . . . brilliant.

In our house, poaching eggs (page 25) without using apple cider vinegar is illegal—we even sneak a dash into apple pie filling to brighten it. It makes a great salad dressing, and we often add a splash to soups or braised dishes if the flavors need a little lifting up. A great trick.

BALSAMIC VINEGAR
(Giuseppe Giusti) Most people use balsamic vinegar on tomatoes (it's an Italian thing), but have you had balsamic vinegar with avocado? A DREAM combination. It's definitely the most abstract vinegar there is because of its distinct color and almost sweet taste.

RICE WINE VINEGAR
(Mizkan Nakano) The mellow note of rice wine vinegar is so nice when mixed with fresh lime or lemon juice for a deep, fruity acid. It's so good on fresh fruit or raw vegetables for nibbling. Unlike most vinegars that are made from wine, rice wine vinegar is made from fermented rice. Cool. The yeast changes the sugars in the rice into alcohol. That alcohol is then turned into acid. That's why the vinegar is mellow and sweet.

OLIVE OIL (Colavita or Monini) Olive oil is a mandatory ingredient in our kitchen. We use extra-virgin olive oil, which is also sometimes called the first cold pressing. This means the olives have been pressed for their oil and not heated or twice pressed. It's this "extra virgin" oil that tastes

the best and costs the most. Its flavor is almost fruity, but it's also almost nutty and super tasty on everything. It's not a neutral ingredient; it has personality.

SESAME OIL (Sushi Chef) Sesame oil can sometimes be overpowering, but for some reason, when shallots or scallions are fried in sesame oil, the taste is like whispering the right words at just the right moment.

NONSTICK COOKING SPRAY (Vegalene) Nonstick cooking spray is the best option for cooking the most notorious food: eggs. It's like an insurance policy, so your food won't stick to the pan!

WINES + SPIRITS

RICE WINE (Mizkan Nakano or Momofuku) Rice wine is different from rice wine vinegar (see page 17). It can come in the form of **mirin** and **sake**. We use both in our cooking (most often we use Japanese rice wine, though Chinese rice wine works, too). They offer subtle and delicate flavors that will change your food forever and for the better. They give slightly fermented and sweet notes at the same time. They can taste as if a sweet dried

apricot had crashed into a slightly funky piece of cheese.

CONDIMENTS + SAUCES

DIJON MUSTARD (Maille or Grey Poupon) Dijon mustard is a staple ingredient and can act as a natural thickener, adding body to a sauce, dressing, soup, or stew as well as delivering great taste. A mustardy vinaigrette spooned over roasted carrots or roasted peppers is absolutely amazing—or try stirring a scoop of Dijon into a beef stew for brightness.

CREAMY HORSERADISH (Inglehoffer) Horseradish is a tingly, slightly spicy ingredient—like a cool cousin of Dijon mustard. A shrimp cocktail and raw oysters/clams are great with horseradish. It's also excellent with raw vegetables like radishes and carrots or with the classic pairing—a roast beef sandwich.

SOY SAUCE (Kikkoman) Soy sauce is really good in a vinaigrette or added to noodle dishes and fried rice because it makes food taste like it took hours to cook and develop such rich flavor. Low-sodium soy is worth buying because you can

add more without risking oversalting/overpowering the other flavors.

CHILI CRUNCH (Momofuku) Fried shallots and garlic plus sesame seeds and Korean chili flakes make this spicy, pungent sauce an incredible combination of exciting textures. A small scoop from the jar can add spark to any dish. Pretty cool. Be careful, though, it can get spicy! Though the sweetness of the crunchy shallots and garlic *does* mellow the heat from the chili flakes.

OUR FAVORITE CREAMY, RICH INGREDIENTS

COCONUT MILK (Thai Kitchen) Coconut milk (we use full-fat) adds creaminess without dairy and is definitely a go-to ingredient for a panang or green curry—and desserts, of course. Or make carbonated coconut soda with coconut milk, honey or simple syrup, and club soda. It's lighter on fat and less heavy than cream but equally rich and slightly sweet, too.

BUTTER (Land o' Lakes for baking and Kerrygold for savory cooking) Butter on toast: this is how you start to know which butter brands speak to your taste buds. In our fridge, we have Land o' Lakes for its lightness and not super-imposing flavor, making it especially good for baking. For a fancy, high-fat European butter, we choose Irish Kerrygold. It's milky and almost creamy—and excellent in savory cooking.

TAHINI (Joyva) Sesame paste, which is simply pureed sesame seeds, is by far the most delicious use of sesame there is. It's very rich and has that sesame texture with a flavor that's almost like pureed cashews. Very nutty.

TOMATO PRODUCTS

Canned **San Marzano tomatoes** (Pomodori Pelati) San Marzano tomatoes are a very rare type of tomato. They are grown in Italy in volcanic ash–rich soil, making it super rare to see them in their natural, raw state. They have a unique acidity, mixed with sweetness, and a great firm texture.

TOMATO PASTE (Cento) Tomato paste has a strong tomato flavor that has a slight (tasty) canned tomato taste. It's basically tomatoes that have been cooked down

to a concentrated paste. A clove of garlic cooked in a splash of olive oil with tomato paste and a little cream yields a delicious, quickie tomato sauce. Tomato paste is a must for Penne alla Vodka (page 128), one of our house-favorite pasta dishes.

PASTA + BREADCRUMBS

For dried store-bought **pasta**, we keep bucatini (like a thick spaghetti), penne, and tagliatelle (like a narrow fettuccine noodle) in the pantry at all times.

PANKO BREADCRUMBS (Sushi Chef) These are the crunchiest, most delicious breadcrumbs you'll ever have in your life. They are great for chicken cutlets, baked clams, meatloaf, or meatballs and, if you're feeling bold, they're great toasted (on a baking sheet in a 350°F oven until browned, 3 to 5 minutes) and sprinkled on top of cucumbers (page 94).

THE HEAT METER FROM LEAST SPICY TO MOST SPICY

TABASCO This is definitely the most iconic type of hot sauce. Mix with melted butter and use it to glaze crispy-hot chicken

wings or to add a little heat to scrambled eggs or quiche batter the way Ava's grandmother used to do. Tabasco can make your food tastier—not just spicier.

FRANK'S REDHOT and **CRYSTAL** brands are two of the best hot sauces made. They are decently spicy, but they are the type of spicy that adds flavor, not just heat. They also stand out from other types of hot sauces because they're a little thicker and fruitier.

SRIRACHA (Huy Fong) Sriracha has an almost green jalapeño chile flavor. Mix with mayonnaise or add to eggs or ramen.

SAMBAL OELEK (Huy Fong) might be the spiciest of the bunch here. A tiny bit usually provides enough heat, so work your way up the ladder to this one. The seeds give great texture, and it tastes sort of fruity, but it can really blow out other flavors with its spiciness!

BREAKFAST
according to Ava

This is Ava's favorite meal of the day besides dinner. She gets up in the morning, her head often brimming with ideas, and goes to work on her first meal—even on a school day. In this chapter, we included our core favorites. They appear in the order I recommend making them, starting with egg dishes. Mastering eggs, even a simple plate of fried eggs or a tasty scramble, is the first step to mastering breakfast, and here we explore the fundamentals of scrambling, poaching, and baking. Next up, batters and baked goods, from waffles and pancakes to quiche. And because not all breakfasts involve eggs (and sometimes you just need a quick recipe on a weekday before heading to school or work), we include some simple fruity dishes and a smoothie to round out the breakfast table. As we were finishing this chapter, Ava made the biscuits with chili-crunch butter (page 47) that were just . . . wow! So we made sure to include those, too.

prep time: 5 minutes
cook time: 3 to 5 minutes
yield: 2 servings

MIGAS:
tortillas + scrambled eggs

I turn to TikTok for a lot of visual inspo. While my mom flips through a tattered old cookbook she has had for, like, four decades, I watch a step-by-step video, and it's enough to get me out of my chair and digging around in the pantry. I saw this recipe being made by the chef @acooknamedmatt on TikTok. I'd never seen someone cut up tortillas, make them crispy, and then make them "uncrispy" by pouring eggs over them. Could it be that changing a texture makes them even more delicious? I feel like you can taste the corn in the tortilla more this way. Plus, all the ingredients complement each other so well: the tortillas, the seasoned eggs, and the melty American cheese (I love its creamy, mellow flavor and the richness it adds to the eggs—this is not a place for fancy Brie or aged Gouda).

2 tablespoons **extra-virgin olive oil**

3 (6-inch) **corn tortillas**, cut into 1-inch squares

3 large **eggs**, lightly beaten

Kosher salt

Freshly ground **black pepper**

2 slices **American cheese**

Cilantro leaves and **hot sauce** (optional)

1. CRISP THE TORTILLAS: In a medium nonstick skillet, heat the olive oil over medium heat. When the oil begins to smoke lightly, add the tortillas and brown them in the oil, stirring constantly, until they are golden brown and crisp. Turn off the heat.

2. ADD THE EGGS: Using a rubber spatula, stir the eggs and a splash of water into the tortillas, season with salt and pepper, and immediately add the cheese, tearing it into smaller pieces and sprinkling it so it melts evenly and quickly. Put the heat back on low. Stir the eggs gently and constantly, 1 to 2 minutes, until they are no longer runny or wet looking. Take care to scrape the sides and bottom of the pan as they cook to keep the eggs from sticking or cooking less evenly.

3. FINISH: Once the eggs are all firmed into little bunches and not at all liquidy, they're done. Stop stirring and transfer them to two plates so the eggs don't continue to cook in the hot pan. Top with the cilantro and a splash of hot sauce (if using).

TRY THIS

Place two plates on the counter near the stove so you can quickly get the eggs out of the hot pan before they dry out. For me, cilantro and hot sauce (Frank's or Tabasco) are a must, but for you they can be optional.

prep time: 10 minutes
cook time: 5 minutes
yield: 2 servings

POACHED EGGS +
avocado on ciabatta

Once you've mastered scrambling and frying eggs, you can move on to poaching. It's a real accomplishment to land a nicely poached egg with a runny yolk. We live near Sullivan Street Bakery in Manhattan. The proprietor, Jim Lahey, bakes amazing loaves. My grandmother edited his cookbook *My Bread* (he essentially popularized no-knead bread), so I feel a special connection to his breads, especially his ciabatta, which is like the squatter and softer Italian answer to the French baguette. Wonderfully fatty avocado and runny poached eggs combine here to create a silky effect that almost tastes like there's a ton of cheese . . . but there isn't—it's just the avo and runny yolk living their best life together. Why both types of salt? The kosher salt seasons the poaching liquid for the eggs and the flaky salt provides a little crunch and a last burst of seasoning.

1 tablespoon plus 1 teaspoon **red wine vinegar**

Kosher salt

1 large ripe **avocado**, halved, pitted, and peeled

Maldon flaky sea salt

4 large **eggs**

Freshly ground **black pepper**

2 small **ciabatta rolls**, halved and toasted (2 toasted hamburger or hot dog buns, 2 Kaiser rolls, or a 5- to 6-inch-long halved baguette work, too)

1. SIMMER THE LIQUID: Bring a large high-sided pan with about 3 inches of water to a simmer. Add 1 tablespoon of the vinegar and a pinch of kosher salt. (The salt and vinegar help the eggs take shape more easily as you poach them.)

2. PREP THE AVOCADO: On a flat surface, thinly slice the avocado halves the "short" way (crosswise). Season with Maldon salt for crunch and the remaining 1 teaspoon vinegar. (The vinegar enhances the taste of the avocado and helps prevent it from turning brown.)

3. POACH THE EGGS: Crack each egg into a separate small ramekin, bowl, or teacup and set them on the counter next to the stove (this may seem unnecessary—to use so many dishes—but trust me . . . and see Tips for Poaching Eggs, page 26). Hold the ramekin on one side and gently tilt each bowl into the water to drop in the eggs, one by one, making sure to leave some distance between them. Reduce the heat so the water barely simmers. Allow the eggs to cook for 3 to 4 minutes until the whites are firm and turn completely opaque white. Set a kitchen towel on a plate and use a slotted spoon to gently remove the eggs, one by one, to the towel to drain. Season with Maldon salt and pepper.

4. ASSEMBLE: Set the ciabatta halves on two plates. Add half of the avocado to the bottom halves; gently place two of the poached eggs on top of the avocado. Season with a pinch of Maldon salt and gently add the top half of the bread.

(recipe continues)

● For an everything-bagel vibe, add a dash of furikake seasoning to the eggs or sprinkle with sliced scallions.

● Line the bread with halved cherry tomatoes instead of avocado.

● Cook bacon strips, chop them up, and sprinkle over the eggs.

● Place thin slices of prosciutto between the bread and the eggs (bonus: the prosciutto also protects the bread from getting soggy).

● Sprinkle with sliced scallions.

TIPS FOR POACHING EGGS

1 Patience is a virtue. Poaching may take a little practice, so poach your first eggs with a friend or adult.

2 Seasoning the water with salt and vinegar makes the egg white firm up, so the eggs hold their shape better. Don't skip this step!

3 The poaching water should be simmering (not boiling hard)—a hard boil can cause the eggs to become overly firm or overcook more easily.

4 Cracking the eggs into individual bowls or glasses may seem weird. Why dirty a few bowls? You want to cook all the eggs at the same time, and cracking them over the water one after the next is risky. With separate bowls, you have more control and can gently drop them in one by one more easily.

5 Be ready with a slotted spoon and a clean kitchen/paper towel (to remove excess moisture) so you can remove the eggs and have a place for them to land once they are cooked.

6 Oh, yeah: Have fun!

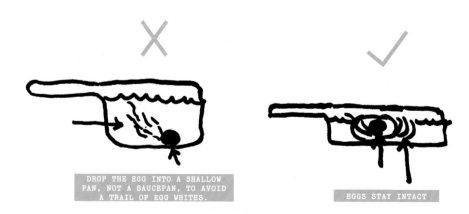

DROP THE EGG INTO A SHALLOW PAN, NOT A SAUCEPAN, TO AVOID A TRAIL OF EGG WHITES.

EGGS STAY INTACT

prep time: 10 minutes
cook time: 20 to 25 minutes (mostly inactive)
yield: 4 or 5 servings

SAUSAGE + EGG FRITTATA

Think of this as the recipe you graduate to once you've mastered the egg scramble and poached eggs and *before* you get to a full omelet. One technique in our family breakfast cookery is gospel: Add water (instead of milk or cream) to whisked eggs for scrambles, omelets, or frittatas. It makes them lighter and fluffier. This water rule applies to all scrambles and all omelets. Egg dishes are a great way to use leftover baked or fried potatoes or other cooked vegetables; you could do that here if you like. I love the slight note of sage from the sausages—it takes me to Thanksgiving stuffing! You start the fritatta on the stovetop and then pop it in the oven for a puffy, pillowy egg dish that's also kind of like a crustless quiche.

1 tablespoon **extra-virgin olive oil**

1 pound **pork breakfast sausage links**, halved lengthwise and sliced

1 large **garlic clove**, minced

8 **sage leaves**

Kosher salt

Nonstick cooking spray

6 large **eggs**

Freshly ground **black pepper**

½ cup grated **Parmesan cheese**

1. Preheat the oven to 325°F. Line a plate with a paper towel.

2. COOK THE SAUSAGES: In a large oven-safe nonstick skillet set over medium heat, heat the olive oil until it starts to smoke lightly. Remove the pan from the heat and add the sausages in a single layer. Return the pan to the heat and brown on the first side for 2 to 3 minutes. Use a pair of kitchen tongs or a spatula to turn each piece on its second side and brown for 2 to 3 minutes more. Stir in the garlic and cook for 30 seconds until fragrant. Use the spatula or a slotted spoon to remove the sausages from the pan and drain on the paper towel–lined plate. Add the sage leaves to the oil remaining in the pan and fry for 1 to 2 minutes until they turn a darker shade of green and are crispy. Sprinkle with salt and use the spatula or a slotted spoon to set them on the plate with the sausages. Use a paper towel to wipe anything sticking to the bottom of the pan and coat with a light layer of nonstick spray as a precaution.

3. GET READY: In a medium bowl, whisk together the eggs, 2 tablespoons cool water, a pinch of salt, and 3 or 4 short turns of pepper. Whisk only enough to integrate the eggs. You don't want to whip too much air into them or make them frothy.

(recipe continues)

4. BAKE: Decrease the heat to medium-low and pour in the egg mixture. Sprinkle with the Parmesan and evenly distribute the sausage and sage. Place the skillet in the center of the oven and allow the eggs to cook, undisturbed until the frittata is cooked through but still slightly soft in the center, 12 to 15 minutes. If still liquidy in the middle, cook for a few minutes more.

5. Place a heat-resistant mat or trivet on the table. Put on an oven mitt or drape a thick kitchen towel over the handle of the pan as you remove the pan of eggs from the oven. (This may be a moment to ask an adult for help.) Place the pan on the mat. Cut the eggs into wedges like a pie and use a spatula to lift the slices up out of the pan and onto people's plates.

prep time: 15 minutes
cook time: 35 to 40 minutes (mostly inactive)
yield: about 3½ cups batter for 6 to 7 waffles
equipment: 7-inch electric waffle maker

AQUAFABA WAFFLES

Don't tell Ava, but in the beginning, I could not be convinced that the liquid from a can of cooked chickpeas, aka aquafaba, could be used in place of whipped egg whites. This recipe proved me wrong—and gets me excited about the chemistry of cooking. And, ironically, this revelation didn't come from one of my favorite cookbooks or magazines—I saw it on TikTok. I have since discovered for myself that when you whip chickpea liquid, magic happens—and whipped aquafaba can truly stand in for whipped egg whites in lots of recipes, from cake batters to meringues and even homemade marshmallows. I like the taste here. The flavor is not particularly strong, and, honestly, it's the mildness of the batter that gives space for other flavors and ingredients, like tasty syrups and sauces or fresh fruit, to shine. The starchiness of the aquafaba gives the waffles structure, and yet this batter is light and the waffles crisp.

2 cups **all-purpose flour**

2 tablespoons **sugar**

2 teaspoons **baking powder**

1 teaspoon **kosher salt**

½ teaspoon ground **cinnamon**

1 cup **whole milk**

1 teaspoon **apple cider vinegar**

1 teaspoon **vanilla extract**

⅔ cup **aquafaba chickpea liquid**
(from a can of chickpeas)

½ stick (4 tablespoons) **unsalted butter**, melted, plus extra for greasing and serving

Maple syrup, for serving

Jam, for serving (optional)

1. Place a baking sheet in the oven and preheat it to 300°F. Plug in the waffle iron and leave it on a flat surface to preheat.

2. MAKE THE BATTER: In a large bowl, combine the flour, sugar, baking powder, salt, and cinnamon. Using a wooden spoon, stir in the milk, vinegar, and vanilla until the batter looks thickened and dense.

3. In the bowl of an electric mixer, fitted with the whisk attachment, whip the aquafaba on medium-high speed until fluffy, 2 to 3 minutes. Stir the melted butter into the batter and then use a rubber spatula to fold in the aquafaba until the ingredients are well combined. Set the batter aside to rest for a few minutes.

4. MAKE THE WAFFLES: Brush the surface of the waffle iron with melted butter. Spoon a generous amount of the batter for each waffle onto the iron (I use about ½ cup of batter per waffle) and cook according to the iron's instructions until the waffles are golden brown and cooked through. You should not see any uncooked batter when you lift the waffle iron to check the waffles. (Be ready with a thick kitchen towel so you protect your hands from the heat of the waffle iron.) Remove the waffles from the iron and transfer to the baking sheet in the oven to keep the waffles warm until all of them are cooked.

5. SERVE: Arrange the waffles on a serving platter or on individual plates. Serve with butter, maple syrup, and jam (if using) on the side.

photographs on pages 32-33

prep time: 20 minutes
cook time: 1 hour (mostly inactive)
yield: 6 to 8 servings

THE SPECIAL CAFÉ QUICHE

My mom and I go to this restaurant right by our apartment that I call the "Special Café" because just about everything they make there is truly next-level delicious. I really love their quiches, so I decided to try coming up with my own version. Even though quiche is very French, I do something super American and add cream cheese to the base of eggs, milk, and Gruyère cheese, which I believe is the secret to its silky, luscious filling. The cream cheese's tang also brings out the smoky and salty flavors of the bacon (or, for a more meaty funkiness, use pancetta in place of the bacon). I also add soy sauce for depth and a bit of Tabasco that heightens the flavors without making the quiche spicy. A wedge of this quiche goes so well with a salad tossed with a super vinegary or mustardy dressing. My mom says this takes her back to her years in Paris. I say it takes me "back" to my childhood.

QUICHE CRUST

1 stick (8 tablespoons) **unsalted butter**, cubed and chilled, plus extra at room temperature for greasing

1½ cups **all-purpose flour**, plus extra for rolling

1 teaspoon **kosher salt**

2 large **egg yolks**

¼ cup **ice water**

QUICHE FILLING

8 thin **bacon strips**, cut crosswise into matchsticks

4 large **eggs**

8 ounces (1 cup) **cream cheese** (not whipped cream cheese), at room temperature

1. Preheat the oven to 400°F. Grease a 9-inch pie dish.

2. MAKE THE DOUGH: In a food processor, pulse the flour and salt to blend. Add the egg yolks and butter and pulse until the mixture comes together (do not overmix or the flour will be overworked and the dough tough once baked). Add 3 tablespoons of the ice water through the feed tube and pulse until the dough comes together into a loose ball (it won't look smooth—it will look a touch dry and crumbly—but if it is too dry, pulse in the remaining 1 tablespoon of ice water). Remove the blade from the food processor and set aside. Gather the dough and turn it onto a floured surface. Press the dough together with your fingers so it feels smooth.

3. ROLL OUT THE DOUGH: Flour the top of the dough and use a rolling pin to roll out the dough into an 11- to 12-inch round. Roll the dough up around the rolling pin and roll it back over the prepared pie dish. Press the dough gently into the bottom and up the sides of the pie dish—ideally, there should be about 1 inch of excess dough hanging over the sides. Pinch the dough up to create a crimped top edge. Gently place a sheet of parchment paper over the crust, fill it with "pie beans" (dried beans or ceramic pie weights), and bake for 12 to 15 minutes or until the edges are lightly browned. Remove the pie dish from the oven and gently lift out the parchment with the beans. Set the crust aside to cool.

(recipe and ingredients continue)

1 cup **whole milk**

2 teaspoons **kosher salt**

½ teaspoon **nutmeg** (preferably freshly grated)

2 teaspoons **soy sauce**

1 teaspoon **Tabasco** (or your fave hot sauce)

4 **scallions** (white and green parts), minced

1½ cups coarsely grated **Gruyère cheese**

½ cup finely grated **Parmesan cheese**

Simple Greens with Mom's 3-2-1-1 Dressing (recipe follows), for serving

4. MAKE THE FILLING: Line a baking sheet with a paper towel. Arrange the bacon matchsticks in a thin layer in a medium skillet over medium heat. Add ¼ cup water (yes, water!) and cook until all the water evaporates, 3 to 5 minutes. (The water will make it less greasy and even crispier. It's a cool trick.) Continue cooking the bacon over medium heat, stirring with a heat-resistant spatula until the bacon crisps completely, 3 to 5 minutes. Use the spatula to transfer the bacon to the prepared baking sheet to drain and cool.

5. In a large bowl, whisk together the eggs, cream cheese, milk, salt, nutmeg, soy sauce, Tabasco, and scallions. Stir in the Gruyère and Parmesan.

6. Place the pie dish with the quiche crust on a baking sheet. Sprinkle half of the bacon evenly on the bottom of the crust, pour in the filling, and sprinkle with the remaining bacon.

7. BAKE AND SERVE: Bake the quiche on the baking sheet until the filling sets (it won't jiggle in the middle) and browns on top, 25 to 30 minutes. Remove the pan from the oven and set aside to cool for 15 to 20 minutes before slicing and serving with the salad. Or cool completely before serving. The baked quiche can be covered with plastic wrap and refrigerated for up to 2 days—rewarm slightly in a 350°F oven for 15 to 20 minutes before serving.

prep time: 5 minutes
cook time: none
yield: about ½ cup dressing for 2 servings

SIMPLE GREENS
with mom's 3-2-1-1 dressing

This is a classic go-to dressing and makes just enough for a nice salad. Use any salad green mix from the supermarket. The dressing easily doubles or triples if you're making salad for a crowd.

3 tablespoons **extra-virgin olive oil**

2 tablespoons **red wine vinegar**

1 tablespoon **Dijon mustard**

1 tablespoon **cool water**

2 cups **mixed greens** (such as arugula and red oak lettuce)

1. MAKE THE DRESSING: In a medium bowl, whisk together the olive oil, vinegar, mustard, and water.

2. MAKE THE SALAD: In a large bowl, toss the greens with half of the dressing and taste for seasoning. Add more dressing if you like it a little saucier or leave as is for a lighter salad. Refrigerate the remaining dressing in an airtight container to use at another time (it keeps for up to 1 week).

prep time: 15 minutes
cook time: 6 to 8 minutes per batch
yield: about 7 cups batter for 16 to
18 (3-inch) pancakes

FLUFFY BEYOND PANCAKES

The funny thing about my house is that while my mom and I are both super into food and recipes, our inspo comes from different sources—you'll usually find my mom flipping through old cookbooks and thinking about Julia Child, while I watch cool cooking videos on my phone. Our family cooking repertoire is a mix of both our styles—but these super-fluffy Japanese-style pancakes are completely *me.* I first saw them on TikTok, and I can confidently say that they're almost as exciting as making cake for breakfast! While you can make the batter a little in advance (no more than 1 hour for ultimate fluff), do not let the batter sit—it will lose its airiness. I believe that a lot of maple syrup is required for pouring on top. But you could skip the syrup and simply double the amount of sugar in the batter for a sweeter cakey pancake. You can also cut this recipe in half to make a smaller batch.

3 cups **full-fat buttermilk**

1 stick (8 tablespoons) **unsalted butter**, melted and cooled slightly

2 teaspoons **vanilla extract**

2 teaspoons **kosher salt**

2 large **egg yolks**, lightly beaten, plus 6 large **egg whites**

3 cups **all-purpose flour**

½ cup **confectioners' sugar**

1 tablespoon plus 1 teaspoon **baking powder**

½ teaspoon **cream of tartar**

Nonstick cooking spray

Lots of **Spiced Maple Syrup** (recipe follows) or **plain maple syrup**

1. START THE BATTER: In a large bowl, whisk together the buttermilk, butter, vanilla, salt, and egg yolks. Set a fine strainer or sieve over the bowl and add the flour, sugar, and baking powder, sifting them into the buttermilk mixture. Use a rubber spatula to gently stir the dry ingredients into the wet until fully mixed.

2. Preheat the oven to 300°F. Place a baking sheet in the oven.

3. WHIP THE EGG WHITES: In the bowl of an electric mixer fitted with the whisk attachment, whip the egg whites and cream of tartar on medium speed until soft peaks form, 4 to 5 minutes. Using a rubber spatula, gently fold the whites into the batter.

4. MAKE THE PANCAKES: Spray a large nonstick skillet with nonstick spray and set the pan over medium heat. Use a ⅓-cup measure to scoop out some batter and add it to the skillet. Repeat, leaving space between the pancakes so they can spread as they cook. Reduce the heat to medium-low and cook the pancakes for 2 to 3 minutes, or until they brown on the first side. Use a spatula to turn them over and cook until golden brown on the other side, an additional 2 to 3 minutes. Transfer the pancakes to the baking sheet in the oven while you make the rest of the pancakes. Serve with lots of maple syrup.

(recipe continues)

SPICED MAPLE SYRUP

prep time: none
cook time: 2 to 3 minutes
yield: 1 cup

This is fun to make because it smells so good as it bubbles and comes together on the stove. The cinnamon and ginger add a spiced flavor to the maple that reminds me of mulled apple cider. Store it in the fridge to drizzle over leftover pancakes, waffles, or cakes, or to make buttered toast feel a little extra.

¾ cup **maple syrup**

¼ cup **apple juice** or **cider**

2 **cinnamon sticks**

1 teaspoon ground **cinnamon**

1 teaspoon ground **ginger**

In a small saucepan, combine the syrup and juice over medium heat. Add the cinnamon sticks, ground cinnamon, and ginger, bring to a simmer, about 3 minutes, then turn off the heat and let cool slightly before serving.

prep time: 5 minutes
cook time: 1 to 2 minutes
yield: 2 servings

ACAI BOWL
with Honey-Toasted Cacao

Acai comes from a type of palm tree—it's a berry that tastes as if pomegranates and blueberries became besties in the last year of high school. I first tried it in a breakfast bowl that I got from a certain favorite spot in NYC (while Mom stayed home with her bowl of boring oatmeal). I was so into it that I started making my own; this is easy because you can buy acai puree at the grocery store in frozen ready-to-use packs. This recipe is exactly how I like it—smooth and balanced. Top with tart, seedy, textured fruits like kiwis and raspberries that balance super sweet ones like bananas. Also think about balancing textures—like starchy bananas or papayas with juicy strawberries. Feel free to experiment with your favorite fruits—I'll add cantaloupe or honeydew in the summertime or use blackberries or raspberries instead of blueberries if they look good. Depending on the sweetness of your acai puree, you may need to add extra honey (acai can be tart, and almost *too* tart, when mixed with underripe fruits).

1 frozen **banana**, cut crosswise into ½-inch-thick slices

1 cup frozen **strawberries**

7 ounces frozen **acai puree**

1 cup **pomegranate juice**

2 tablespoons **smooth peanut butter**

2 tablespoons **honey**

2 tablespoons **cacao nibs**

¼ cup shredded **unsweetened coconut**

1. MAKE THE BOWL: In a blender, combine half of the banana, the strawberries, acai puree, pomegranate juice, peanut butter, and 1 tablespoon of the honey. Blend on medium speed until smooth. Do not overmix.

2. BLOOM THE CACAO NIBS: In a medium sauté pan, warm the remaining 1 tablespoon honey over medium heat until it bubbles and froths. Add the cacao nibs and cook for 1 minute, stirring, so they warm and absorb some honey (don't expect the nibs to melt). Set aside.

3. FINISH: Spoon the acai mixture into two medium-size deep bowls. Top with the remaining banana slices, coconut, and warmed honey and cacao nibs.

Cacao Nibs

Cacao nibs are small pieces of crushed cacao beans that are used to make chocolate. The nibs are pleasantly bitter and have a great crunchy texture. They give this a subtle chocolate note that is tasty with all the fruits. A cool tip is to "bloom" them in hot honey (or even butter) before using—the heat brings out their flavor (kind of like toasting spices), and the honey sweetens them up.

prep time: 10 minutes
cook time: none
yield: 2 servings

DRAGON FRUIT SALAD
with lime

While I *know* I saw dragon fruit in the supermarket and found it so beautiful that I had to try it (it's intensely fuchsia colored on the outside and white and black polka dot inside), my mom insists I first saw it on *Chopped* (eye roll). There are two kinds of dragon fruit: white, which I find mild in flavor, and the red kind that tastes like a cross between a prickly pear and a juicy mango. If you can't find dragon fruit, sub in the same amount of cubed ripe mango, papaya, or pineapple. Chili powder is a cool addition because it adds a smoky note and a slight tingle of heat. Feel free to omit it, but it's great with the tart lime and that tiny pop of grassiness and tartness from the blueberries.

1 decently sized red or white **dragon fruit**, peeled

1 pint **blueberries**

Juice of 1 small **lime**

1 teaspoon **sugar**

½ teaspoon **chili powder**

½ teaspoon **kosher salt**

1 teaspoon **honey**

1. PREP THE DRAGON FRUIT: Slice the dragon fruit in half and dice it into small cubes. Place in a medium bowl. Add the blueberries.

2. MAKE THE VINAIGRETTE AND SERVE: In a separate small bowl, whisk together the lime juice, sugar, chili powder, and salt. Drizzle the vinaigrette and the honey over the fruit and serve.

TRY THIS

To juice limes more easily, let them sit out at room temperature before juicing instead of trying to juice them straight from a cold fridge.

healthy but good smoothie, page 46

prep time: 5 minutes
cook time: none
yield: 1 serving

HEALTHY BUT GOOD SMOOTHIE

This smoothie came about because my two closest friends like to put maple syrup on fresh snow and eat it like ice cream. I took the inspo to add maple syrup to a smoothie from them. The result is a blended drink that's healthy without tasting basic. The sleeper in here? Pear. My mom is always talking about how pears are someday going to become more chic than apples. Okay. Well, I don't know about that—I just know that pears are starchy, crunchy, and light all at the same time. Chia seeds are loaded with antioxidants and fiber and add fun texture. Feel free to sub in any melon or mango for the pear, and blackberries for the blueberries.

1 ripe **Bosc** or **Anjou pear**, cored

1 cup fresh or frozen **blueberries**

1 cup chilled unsweetened **apple juice**

1 cup **ice**

1 tablespoon **maple syrup**

2 tablespoons **chia seeds**

In a blender, combine the pear, blueberries, apple juice, ice, and maple syrup on low speed until smooth. Taste. Stir in the chia seeds, set aside for 5 minutes to hydrate the chia, then pour into a glass.

photograph on page 44

prep time: 15 to 20 minutes
(plus 2 hours for the
biscuits to freeze)
cook time: 35 minutes
(mostly inactive)
yield: 14 biscuits and
⅔ cup chili-crunch butter

CHEDDAR BISCUITS
with chili-crunch butter

The best way to get to know a new ingredient is to start experimenting—here, I took some chili-crunch oil (a *wickedly* tasty condiment made from dried chiles, spices, and garlic—it tastes like a bag of the best BBQ potato chips mixed with garlic) from a Momofuku gift box my mom gave me for Christmas, and I added it to noodles and savory pancakes (page 103) before parking it with biscuits and spicy butter as I do here. During my cooking experiments, I discovered that I love the texture *and* the spice of chili crunch, so I decided to blend the chili crunch *into* the butter for the biscuits rather than just drizzling it over them (the butter is also excellent on top of roasted vegetables or fish). Try a little at first and see what you think. If you aren't into it, the good news is that you can also just eat the biscuits with plain butter.

CHEDDAR BISCUITS

1¾ cups **all-purpose flour**, plus extra for shaping

2 tablespoons **baking powder**

1 tablespoon **sugar**

2 teaspoons **kosher salt**

1 teaspoon **baking soda**

2 sticks (16 tablespoons) **unsalted butter**, cubed and chilled

⅓ cup cold **full-fat buttermilk**

½ cup grated **Cheddar cheese**

1. MAKE THE BISCUIT DOUGH: Line a baking sheet with parchment paper. In a large bowl, whisk together the flour, baking powder, sugar, salt, and baking soda. Add the butter cubes and work them in with your fingers until the mixture resembles wet, coarse sand, with the butter no larger than small peas. Switch to a wooden spoon (or use your hands) to stir in the buttermilk and cheese. Mix until the dough looks smooth and the ingredients are well combined.

2. SHAPE THE BISCUITS: Transfer the dough to a flat, floured surface and use your hands to flatten the dough to a 2-inch thickness. Use a 2-inch round cutter to cut out 14 biscuits, cutting them close together to make as little scrap as possible. Arrange the biscuits on the prepared baking sheet and freeze for at least 2 hours or up to 24 hours.

3. Preheat the oven to 375°F.

4. BAKE: Place the baking sheet in the oven and bake the biscuits for 25 minutes or until the tops are golden brown.

(recipe and ingredients continue)

CHILI-CRUNCH BUTTER

5 tablespoons **unsalted butter**, softened

2 medium **shallots**, minced (about ⅓ cup)

1 teaspoon **kosher salt**

A few grates of **lemon zest** (see Zesting Lemons), plus 2 teaspoons fresh **lemon juice**

1 tablespoon **chili crunch**

1 tablespoon **honey**

1 tablespoon **Maldon flaky sea salt**

2 tablespoons finely chopped **flat-leaf parsley**

5. MAKE THE CHILI-CRUNCH BUTTER: In a medium sauté pan, melt 1 tablespoon of the butter over medium-low heat and add the shallots. Cook until translucent but not browned, 3 to 5 minutes.

6. Transfer the shallots to a medium bowl. Stir the kosher salt, lemon zest, and lemon juice into the warm shallots. Use a fork to blend in the remaining 4 tablespoons butter. Stir in the chili crunch, honey, flaky salt, and parsley. Taste for seasoning. Serve the hot biscuits with the butter on the side.

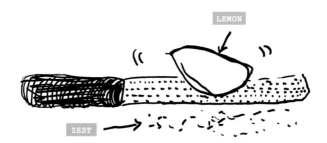

ZESTING LEMONS

Zesting *just* the outer layer of the lemon gives you all the oil and floral notes—the white pithy part can be bitter, so don't zest it. We use a Microplane grater and move it all around the lemon, zesting gently to remove the surface. Keep in mind that there is such a thing as too much zest. Our general rule is you get about 1 tablespoon of zest and about 2 tablespoons of juice from 1 lemon.

LUNCH BOX

When I was growing up, my biggest wish was for my lunch not to be too weird or embarrassing. My mother (Ava's grandmother) was the queen of sending me to school with dinner leftovers like meatballs with tomato sauce wrapped in a (leaky, messy) aluminum foil package or roasted chicken with a grainy mustard dressing and leftover romaine salad with croutons. Delicious? Yes. Did everyone look at me like I was a weirdo? Yes. Did anyone ever want to trade lunches with me? Nope. Times have changed, though.

Ava's generation appreciates home-cooked food, and the sophistication level of her lunches goes far beyond anything I ever wanted. I just craved PB&J with the crusts cut off. Ava has other ideas, and they are varied and exciting. There are hints of the cooking influences she has grown up around (French, Italian, NYC's delicious ramen spots), but there is so much more. Whether you want to try something ambitious and exciting like, Vegetable Summer Rolls (page 54), or crave a tasty Roasted Vegetable Sandwich (page 58), you'll find plenty of fun ideas and a great, low-risk way (because we often prepare our own lunches and serve as our own lunch box guinea pigs) to work on developing your own culinary point of view.

prep time: 20 to 25 minutes
cook time: 5 minutes
yield: 10 to 12 rolls

VEGETABLE SUMMER ROLLS

This is a Mom recipe that turned into an Ava signature that was definitely inspired by the Vietnamese summer rolls we have eaten in restaurants. Think of making these vegetable-stuffed rice paper rolls like making a wrap, burrito, or filled crepe. There are a few tricks to making them a very easy project. The rice papers (sold in a circle stack at most supermarkets) need to be dipped quickly in warm water, one by one, as you are making the rolls. Also, the papers are simple enough to use, but they don't appreciate sitting around once they are moistened. Also, don't overfill them, and for the first few, even go spare on the filling until you get the hang of it. (As a side note, I always buy an extra package of rice papers to have on hand—they're also delicious just fried until crispy and eaten like a chip!) If you want to add some protein, feel free to mix sliced cooked chicken or cooked shrimp into the filling.

ROLLS

Half of an 8-ounce package of
vermicelli rice noodles
(like Taste of Thai brand)

¼ cup **rice wine vinegar**

2 tablespoons **sesame seeds**

2 tablespoons **fish sauce**

2 tablespoons low-sodium
soy sauce

1 tablespoon
dark brown sugar

1 large **carrot**, julienned into
matchsticks (about 1 cup)

1 **English cucumber**,
peeled and cut into very
thin rounds (about 1 cup)

1 cup **mixed greens**,
finely chopped

12 to 14 (8½-inch) sheets of
rice paper (we like Banh Trang
Vietnamese and Dynasty
brands)

20 to 24 **mint leaves**

30 to 36 **basil leaves**

SAUCE

½ cup **smooth peanut butter**

1 tablespoon low-sodium
soy sauce

1 tablespoon
rice wine vinegar

1 large **garlic clove**,
grated

1 tablespoon finely
grated **ginger**

(recipe continues)

1. COOK THE NOODLES: Follow the package instructions to cook the vermicelli until al dente, usually 4 to 5 minutes. Drain, rinse under cool water, and then coarsely chop (you should have about 1 cup).

2. MAKE THE FILLING: In a large bowl, whisk together the vinegar, sesame seeds, fish sauce, soy sauce, and brown sugar. Add the noodles and toss so they absorb the flavors. Stir in the carrot, cucumber, and mixed greens and toss lightly.

3. ASSEMBLE THE ROLLS: Cover a flat, dry surface with a kitchen towel and set a medium bowl filled about halfway with warm water off to the side. Submerge a sheet of rice paper in the water for a few seconds and use both hands to remove it and lay it out flat on top of the kitchen towel. Place 2 mint leaves and 3 basil leaves along the length of the rice paper and top with some filling, leaving about 1 inch empty on either end. Fold the bottom of the paper up and over the filling, fold each end of the paper inward, and then roll it up like a burrito. Set the roll on a serving platter and repeat with the remaining papers and filling.

4. MAKE THE SAUCE: In a medium bowl, whisk together the peanut butter, soy sauce, vinegar, and garlic with ¼ cup warm water until smooth. Whisk in the ginger, taste for seasoning, and serve alongside the rolls. Store leftover rolls (if there are any!) covered in plastic wrap in the fridge. They are best eaten the same day they are made.

THIS IS MY DAD'S CLEAVER. AVA AND I HAVE SO MANY KITCHEN TOOLS THAT ARE SENTIMENTAL TO US. USING THEM MAKES US FEEL LIKE OUR LOVED ONES ARE STILL WITH US. TREASURE YOUR HAND-ME-DOWNS.

prep time: 15 minutes
cook time: 30 minutes
yield: 4 sandwiches and
about ½ cup dressing

ROASTED VEGETABLE
SANDWICH
with tahini-coriander dressing

This is a Mom recipe that I've adopted as my own. My mom learned about mixing the rich, silky sesame flavors of tahini with roasted vegetables when she was working in the south of France. I just like the combo because it's tasty. I make this sandwich in the early fall with the vegetables that are available at the farmers' market, like eggplant, red bell peppers, and zucchini. I char them to make them extra sweet and flavorful and then drizzle it all with lots of tahini dressing, which totally makes this sandwich because of its smooth sesame and pungent garlicky taste. I add aromatic coriander (see page 16), too, and the combination of the sauce, pillowy pita bread, and silky bitter-charred and sweet roasted veg is out-of-this-world amazing. Like I said, I'm no veggie connoisseur, but this could *maybe* turn me into one (not likely . . . but *maybe*). The charring of the peppers is a life-changing step—I also like the way the charring makes the peppers extra sweet. If you don't have a gas burner, feel free to use store-bought roasted peppers.

VEGETABLES + SANDWICH

6 tablespoons
extra-virgin olive oil,
plus extra for greasing

2 large **garlic cloves**, minced

1 large **eggplant**,
cut into 1-inch rounds

1 medium **zucchini**,
cut into 1-inch rounds

Kosher salt

Freshly ground **black pepper**

2 large **red bell peppers**

2 tablespoons
balsamic vinegar

4 **pita breads**, opened halfway
(not completely split
into two halves)

DRESSING

6 tablespoons
(generous ⅓ cup)
tahini

Juice of 1 large **lemon**

1 tablespoon **honey**

1 teaspoon **coriander seeds**,
toasted

1. Preheat the oven to 375°F. Line a baking sheet with aluminum foil and brush the foil with olive oil.

2. COOK THE EGGPLANT AND ZUCCHINI: In a large bowl, mix together 4 tablespoons of the olive oil and the garlic. Toss the eggplant and zucchini rounds in the oil and season with a few pinches of salt and a few turns of pepper. Arrange the rounds in a single layer on the prepared baking sheet, season with salt and pepper, and bake for 15 to 20 minutes or until a fork slides easily into the middle of the vegetables without any resistance.

3. CHAR THE PEPPERS: Place the red peppers directly on the flame of a burner on low heat. Allow the skin of the peppers to char (turn black) and as the skin begins to turn color, use a pair of heat-resistant metal tongs to rotate them often until all sides are charred. Use the tongs to remove the peppers from the heat (be careful—if you squeeze the pepper too hard, it will split and the liquid will leak all over the place!) and set them aside to cool for a couple of minutes. Cut them in half and remove the stem parts and seeds from the insides. Place the halves, cut side down, on a flat surface and use a clean kitchen towel to wipe the charred skin from the pepper flesh. Finely chop the pepper halves, add them to a medium bowl, and toss with the vinegar.

4. MAKE THE DRESSING: In a medium bowl, whisk together the tahini and the lemon juice with the honey, coriander, and remaining 2 tablespoons olive oil. Add 1 teaspoon salt and taste for seasoning, adding more honey if it's missing sweetness or a last squeeze of lemon if it needs brightness and acidity.

5. ASSEMBLE: On a flat surface, open each pita pocket and use a spoon to spread some of the tahini dressing on the bottom half of the bread. Next, divide the eggplant and zucchini evenly among the pita, then stuff some peppers into each pita. Drizzle the dressing over the vegetables and close the pita. Press down gently on each sandwich to tighten the layers, and eat!

prep time: 15 minutes
(plus 2 hours to chill shrimp)
cook time: 5 to 8 minutes
yield: 4 to 6 servings

SHRIMP COCKTAIL

I think we develop our own cooking style a lot from watching our parents—and then often deciding what *not* to do! My mom always has a bottle of vinegar out on the counter, and I think that's why I am always turning to that and other strong flavors like horseradish and garlic (both used here in the cocktail sauce) to pack a punch in my recipes. The cocktail sauce is a combination of ketchup's sweetness and tang (yes, I love ketchup) with the bite of horseradish (get the creamy kind and not the other ones that are kind of stringy and overly vinegary). Add a little lemon juice and Worcestershire and you have the classic dip for poached shrimp (sounds fancy—but *so* easy). If I were making this cocktail sauce right now, I know my mom would come by and add a huge splash of red wine vinegar to it. Personally, though, I prefer rice wine vinegar for a mellower, sweeter note.

And let's talk about bay leaves. My mom loves them and uses them in a lot of recipes, like slow-cooker beef stew, or in a homemade chicken stock. I've learned to love their flavor of mint and pine trees. I like that taste against the mild and sweet shrimp.

SHRIMP

1 large **lemon**, halved

4 dried **bay leaves**

2 tablespoons **kosher salt**

2 teaspoons **Tabasco**

2 pounds (32 to 40 shrimp per pound) raw **shrimp**, shelled and deveined, tail-on, fresh or thawed if frozen

SAUCE

1 cup **ketchup**

¼ cup creamy **horseradish**

¼ cup **rice wine vinegar**

2 teaspoons **Worcestershire sauce**

Juice of 1 medium **lemon**

1 teaspoon **Tabasco**

1 teaspoon coarsely ground **black pepper**

Kosher salt

(recipe continues)

1. PREPARE THE SHRIMP: In a large saucepan, combine 2½ quarts (10 cups) water, the lemon halves, bay leaves, salt, and Tabasco. Stir to blend and bring to a simmer. Remove the pan from the heat and let cool for a few minutes. Add the shrimp and allow them to sit in the liquid, off the heat, until they turn pink and are cooked in the middle, 3 to 5 minutes. Use a slotted spoon to remove the shrimp and drain on a kitchen towel. Refrigerate for at least 2 hours and up to 24 hours.

2. MAKE THE SAUCE: In a large bowl, whisk together the ketchup, horseradish, vinegar, Worcestershire, lemon juice, Tabasco, and pepper. Season with salt and taste. If it needs more acid, add more vinegar or lemon juice. If it needs more zing, add a squirt more horseradish or a dash more Tabasco. Sometimes this sauce needs a little adjusting, and this is a good place to develop that skill in finding the flavors and making it taste the way you like!

3. SERVE: If eating lunch at home, transfer the sauce to a bowl for dunking and serve the shrimp on the side. If eating lunch on the go, pack the shrimp in a resealable plastic bag and put the sauce in a separate small container or zip-top bag.

What Is Poaching?

We have already seen poaching (gently cooking an ingredient in simmering liquid) in the breakfast chapter (see poached eggs, page 25). But you can poach many things. Poaching is nice because it's a cooking method that produces a light and not-at-all greasy end result. Shrimp, chicken breasts, and tuna and salmon fillets are all great poached.

prep time: 5 minutes
(plus 20 minutes for marinating eggs)
cook time: 15 to 18 minutes
yield: 2 servings

SOUPED-UP CHICKEN RAMEN

I love the instant chicken-flavored ramen soup packages from the supermarket—during the winter, they make a fast and tasty thermos lunch to bring to school. My mom said she used to make them in a hot pot in her dorm room in college and added nothing to them! (Honestly, it's sometimes surprising she became a chef.) I always add extras like fresh herbs, a sprinkle of ground ginger, and thinly sliced radishes or carrots to make it more like a bowl of ramen that I'd get in a restaurant. If we have leftover roasted chicken or cooked shrimp in the fridge, I mix that in. I bring this to school in a container that keeps it hot, and I appreciate it so much during the colder months. Opening the lid makes me feel like I'm home for lunch and taking a breather from my day. The soy-egg technique is great as a stand-alone snack, too. The soy sauce seeps into the egg and makes it deeply tasty. You can use the eggs as a topping for salads as well or sneak some into a BLT sandwich.

2 large **eggs**

1 tablespoon low-sodium **soy sauce**

1 package **chicken-flavored ramen**

½ pound ground **chicken**

1 tablespoon grated **ginger**

2 **scallions** (white and green parts), minced

1 tablespoon **rice wine vinegar**

1 tablespoon fresh **lime juice**

1. COOK THE EGGS: Gently place the eggs in a medium pot and cover them with cold water. Bring the water to a rolling boil over high heat. When the water boils, remove the pot from the heat, cover, and let the eggs stand for 10 minutes. Meanwhile, pour the soy sauce onto a plate. Gently pour off the hot water and run cool water over the eggs to stop them from cooking further. Peel the eggs. If necessary, rinse them quickly under cool water to remove any small shell bits and dry them off thoroughly. Cut them in half and place them, yolk side down, on the plate with the soy sauce so they marinate for 10 minutes. Take them out of the soy sauce and set aside on another plate until ready to eat. (Leaving them in the soy too long leaves them oversalted. But hold onto the soy for serving.)

2. MAKE THE BROTH AND NOODLES: Heat 1½ cups water and add the ramen seasoning packet. Bring to a simmer over medium heat and add the chicken, ginger, scallions, vinegar, and lime juice. Taste for seasoning, adjust as needed, and add the noodles. Simmer over low heat until the noodles are cooked, 5 to 8 minutes.

3. FINISH: Spoon the broth and noodles into two bowls and top with the egg halves and reserved soy sauce.

photographs on pages 64–65

prep time: 10 minutes (plus at least 30 minutes for marinating)
cook time: about 30 minutes
yield: 2 servings

MISO-GLAZED SALMON BOWL
with rice + cucumber

I like this bowl a lot. The marinated salmon makes it vibrant, the rice makes it filling, and the cucumbers make it delicious. I prepare this the night before and pack the fish separately. If I know lunch will be at a late time, I pack the fish in a little ice to keep it cold until I eat. Otherwise, I keep everything at room temperature. You can sub in cooked shrimp or other types of fish here. You can also add roasted vegetables (take the ones from the sandwich on page 58) and make this a vegetarian rice bowl. The rice is the vibe for me. It's like a sushi bar flavor because the rice is seasoned. Most people don't think about adding anything to rice, but a tiny tweak can take it to the next level. Let that be one of our many cooking secrets that gives us an edge in the kitchen.

¾ cup **long-grain white rice** (preferably jasmine)

Kosher salt

1 **lime**

½ cup **mirin rice wine**

1 tablespoon **sugar**

1 tablespoon **sesame seeds**

1 small **English cucumber**, cut into thin rounds

2 tablespoons blond/white **miso paste**

1 tablespoon low-sodium **soy sauce**

1 tablespoon **canola oil**, plus extra for cooking the salmon

2 (4-ounce) portions of **salmon**, skin on, pinbones removed

1. Preheat the oven to 375°F.

2. COOK AND SEASON THE RICE: Bring 1½ cups water to a boil in a medium oven-safe saucepan. Stir in the rice and a pinch of salt and return the pan to a boil over medium-high heat. Turn off the heat, cover, and place the pan in the oven to cook until the rice is tender and has absorbed all the liquid, 12 to 14 minutes. Carefully remove the pan from the oven and immediately mix the rice with 5 or 6 light grates of zest from the lime. Cover and set aside.

3. MARINATE THE CUCUMBERS: In a medium bowl, combine the mirin with the sugar and sesame seeds. Add the cucumber, cover the bowl with plastic wrap, and marinate in the refrigerator for 30 minutes and up to 2 days.

4. MARINATE THE SALMON: Juice the lime into another medium bowl and add the miso, soy sauce, and oil, whisking to combine. Arrange the salmon pieces, skin side up, on a baking sheet lined with parchment paper and spoon the marinade over the fish. Cover and refrigerate for 30 minutes and up to 4 hours.

5. Preheat the oven to 350°F.

6. COOK THE SALMON: Remove the salmon from the marinade (discard the parchment and save the marinade in the baking sheet and set it aside) and place the fish, skin side down, on a kitchen towel to dry the skin slightly. Heat a medium oven-safe nonstick

(recipe continues)

skillet over medium heat and add 2 tablespoons of oil. When the oil begins to smoke lightly, remove the pan from the heat. Place the fish, skin side down, in the pan and return the pan to the stove. Cook for 2 to 3 minutes over medium heat to allow the skin to crisp up. Place the pan in the oven and roast the salmon until it is cooked through, 6 to 8 minutes more. The salmon is cooked when it turns a light pink-orange color and is no longer transparent-looking in the middle. (If the salmon gets white around the edges and sides, it's a sign that it is starting to overcook.) Carefully remove the pan from the oven and set aside.

7. FINISH: Set the pan with the marinade over medium-high heat and bring to a boil. Let it bubble for 2 minutes, until slightly thickened, then pour it over the fish.

8. ASSEMBLE: If taking to go, divide the zesty rice between two bowls with fitted lids and arrange the pickled cucumbers around the rice. Divide the salmon and any excess cooking liquid between the two bowls. You can remove and discard the skin if you don't want to include it. Alternatively, cool the fish for 15 to 20 minutes and pack it in a separate container from the rice.

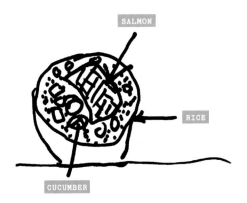

prep time: 10 minutes
cook time: 15 minutes
yield: 4 to 6 servings

DAN DAN NOODLES

This was one of my grandma's favorite Sichuan dishes. She used to order it every time we got takeout from her favorite local Chinese restaurant and was the type of person who knew the difference between flavors and dishes of various regions of China, as filtered through the menus of NYC restaurants, and dan dan noodles was her absolute favorite. I would always steal a bite or two, almost afraid of how spicy it would be. She loved the punch of garlic and tingly heat of Sichuan peppercorns that this dish traditionally has. Well, this is my version. While Chinese sesame paste is traditional, I use tahini instead because it's what we have in the fridge, and for the chili sauce, I like the Fuyun Xiang La Wang brand (because I like the nontoasty flavor here) or sometimes sambal oelek, which is an Indonesian chili sauce. I love Sichuan peppercorns and their tingly heat that my grandma liked, too, but I find 5-spice powder is a little easier to handle. You may think this dish is kind of mellow until you stir in the meat and sauce—then watch out!!! (If you don't like spicy, add only a little or no chili paste.) I make this saucier than it is classically because it's addictive and better when saucy, imho. A few notes: I like to grate the garlic on a Microplane grater so it "melts" in—grating is also faster than chopping (just watch your knuckles). While dan dan is traditionally made with ground pork, you could sub in small, cut, cooked vegetables to make this dish vegetarian and still equally delicious.

DAN DAN SAUCE

¼ cup low-sodium **soy sauce**

2 tablespoons **tahini** or Chinese sesame paste

1 tablespoon **Chinese chili sauce**

2 large **garlic cloves**, grated

2 tablespoons **warm water**

1 tablespoon **sugar**

PORK

½ pound ground **pork**

1 tablespoon **canola oil**

Kosher salt

½ teaspoon **5-spice powder**

1 tablespoon low-sodium **soy sauce**

2 teaspoons **sesame oil**

NOODLES

2 tablespoons **kosher salt**

½ pound fresh **Chinese egg noodles** (traditional choice) or dried udon or dried soba noodles

2 **scallions** (white and green parts), minced

1 cup **baby spinach leaves**

(recipe continues)

1. MAKE THE SAUCE: In a large bowl, whisk together the soy sauce, tahini, chili sauce, garlic, water, and sugar.

2. COOK THE PORK: Separate the pork into small pieces. Heat a large saucepan over medium heat and add the canola oil. When the oil begins to smoke lightly, remove the pan from the heat and sprinkle the pork over the hot oil. Return the pan to the heat and cook, without touching, until the pork browns, 2 to 3 minutes. Stir, sprinkle with 1 teaspoon salt and the 5-spice powder, and stir again. Cook for 2 to 3 minutes more. Remove from the heat and stir in the soy sauce and sesame oil.

3. COOK THE NOODLES: Bring a large pot of water to a rolling boil. Add the salt and return to a rolling boil. Add the noodles and cook, following the package instructions, stirring often with a slotted spoon to make sure they don't clump or stick to the bottom, until they are tender but still have a chewy vibe. Drain the noodles in a large colander, reserving ½ cup of the cooking liquid in case you need it to adjust the flavors of the sauce.

4. FINISH: Stir the scallions, spinach, and seasoned pork into the sauce. Add some cooking liquid if the taste and/or consistency of the sauce isn't to your liking. Dump the noodles into a large serving bowl and pour the sauce over top. Do not toss or stir. It's traditional to let each diner stir all the ingredients together as they dig in to eat.

WE LIKE TO SOMETIMES SPOON THE SAUCE
OVER THE NOODLES AND ADD THE SPINACH
ON TOP—BY NOT FULLY COMBINING THE
DISH, EACH BITE TASTES A LITTLE
DIFFERENT THAN THE LAST.

prep time: 10 minutes
cook time: 30 to 35 minutes
yield: 1 or 2 servings

VEGETABLE FRIED RICE

This vegetable fried rice is great for school lunch, dinner, or even breakfast—and it's so simple. I saw chef Ming Tsai make it in a TikTok video and decided to add peas to my version because every fried rice I've eaten in my life tastes incomplete without peas. The soy sauce is a great addition because it adds so much umami. While my grandmother was not subtle about serving leftovers, I like a meal to taste fresh, as if it's the first time around—and by adding in some leftover cooked vegetables or even roasted meat, you get that. That said, instead of making fresh rice, you can use 1 cup of leftover cooked rice for this recipe—I love the floral, light flavor of basmati the most.

1 cup frozen **peas**

3 tablespoons **unsalted butter**

1 small **yellow onion**, diced small

1 medium **carrot**, grated

Kosher salt

Freshly ground **black pepper**

½ cup **basmati rice**

2 **scallions** (white and green parts), minced

1 tablespoon low-sodium **soy sauce**

2 large **eggs**, lightly beaten

Leaves from 4 sprigs of **basil**

1. Place the peas in a bowl on the counter and set aside to thaw while you make the rice. Line a baking sheet with parchment paper.

2. COOK THE RICE: In a small sauté pan set over medium heat, melt 1 tablespoon of the butter. Add the onion and carrot, season with a generous pinch of salt and a few turns of pepper, and cook, stirring with a wooden spoon, until the onion softens, 3 to 5 minutes. Turn up the heat to high, stir in the rice, and toast it for a minute, stirring continuously. When it starts to make crackling sounds, add 1 cup water. Adjust the heat to very low, cover, and cook until the rice is done, 12 to 14 minutes. Taste a few grains of rice to make sure it is tender but not mushy. It should not be crunchy at all. Use a fork to fluff the rice, and spread it out on the prepared baking sheet to cool.

3. MAKE THE FRIED RICE: In an 8- or 10-inch nonstick skillet over medium-high heat, melt 1½ tablespoons of the butter. Add the rice in an even layer. Turn up the heat to high and cook, untouched, until the rice crackles and browns, 2 to 3 minutes. Stir and then let the rice be until it browns again, 2 to 3 minutes more. Stir in the scallions and thawed peas. Add the soy sauce and stir to combine, continuing to cook until the rice is steaming hot, 2 to 3 minutes. Transfer the rice to a bowl.

4. COOK THE EGGS: Return the same skillet to medium heat and melt the remaining ½ tablespoon butter. Pour in the eggs and cook, stirring gently and constantly, until set, about 2 minutes. Season with a pinch of salt and a turn of pepper. Cook for 15 to 30 seconds more, then stir again, scraping the sides and bottom of the pan to keep the eggs moving. Stir the eggs and the basil into the fried rice. Taste for seasoning and serve.

SANDWICHES, TARTINES + TACOS

This is an extension of lunch ideas from Ava. You'll find sandwiches and cousins of sandwiches—the main driving force is the desire to create deep, memorable flavors and enhance your ability to coax them out of unexpected, simple, and familiar ingredients. That's what gradually makes us better and better cooks, the more we spend time in the kitchen. We are investing in ourselves as home cooks. A splash of pickle juice or vinegar in an unusual spot, for example, can brighten a sandwich you've made and eaten many times in your life. And then it becomes new again.

prep time: 15 minutes
cook time: 35 to 40 minutes
yield: 4 burgers

BURGERS
with onion jam + homemade thousand island

This is a hamburger recipe with at least two generations of Guarnaschellis behind it. When cooking chicken or beef, my mom almost always pulls out the same ingredients: Worcestershire sauce, dry sherry, or mustard. So, this burger mix is inspired by her, with my additions like soy sauce (umami) and American cheese. If I buy the beef preground at the supermarket, I choose an 85/15 blend, or, if I'm feeling fancy, I ask the butcher to grind up an equal combo of sirloin and brisket. If possible, I love a little extra beef fat mixed into the blend. My mom swears by ground sirloin and ground chuck, but find what works best for the flavors you like, be they lean (sirloin) or fatty (chuck), rich (brisket) or grassy (like grass-fed beef)—beef's taste and texture vary from cut to cut. Here, I make a homemade Thousand Island dressing—it's so creamy and sweet—and pair it with a savory caramelized onion jam, which makes it like a drive-thru burger but ten times better. Sometimes I eat a burger with just ketchup and pickles. A burger is a mood, and it can be anything you want to eat without judgment.

ONION JAM

1 tablespoon **canola oil**

2 medium **red onions**, cut into ½-inch rounds

Kosher salt

1 tablespoon **dark brown sugar**

1 tablespoon **red wine vinegar**

THOUSAND ISLAND

3 tablespoons **mayonnaise**

2 tablespoons **ketchup**

1 tablespoon brine from a jar of **cornichons** or **dill pickles**

2 teaspoons **hot sauce**

BURGERS

1½ pounds ground **beef** (85% lean)

2 tablespoons **dry sherry**

1 tablespoon low-sodium **soy sauce**

1 tablespoon **Worcestershire sauce**

1 tablespoon **canola oil**

8 slices **American cheese**

4 seeded **hamburger buns**, halved

1 head of **Romaine lettuce**, coarsely chopped

¼ cup **cornichons**, for serving

(recipe continues)

1. PREPARE THE ONION JAM: Heat a large sauté pan over medium heat. Add the oil, onion slices, and a generous pinch of salt and toss to combine. Decrease the heat to medium-low, add the sugar, and cook, stirring from time to time, until the onions are caramelized and tender, 20 to 25 minutes. Stir in the vinegar and cook for 1 to 2 minutes to allow the vinegar to blend in.

2. MAKE THE THOUSAND ISLAND: In a small bowl, stir together the mayo, ketchup, pickle brine, and hot sauce.

3. MAKE THE PATTIES: In a medium bowl, break up the meat and spread it up the sides of the bowl—this is so the seasoning really permeates the meat with minimal mixing/handling. Add the sherry, soy sauce, and Worcestershire. Mix quickly with your hands to make sure all the flavors get integrated. (Do not overmix—the more you work the meat, the tougher the burger.) Form the meat into four ¾-inch-thick patties.

4. COOK THE BURGERS: Heat a large cast-iron skillet over medium-high heat and add the oil. When the oil begins to smoke lightly, remove the pan from the heat (just slide it onto another burner) and arrange the patties in a single layer in the pan with space between each. Return the pan to the heat and cook, undisturbed, for about 3 minutes. Use a metal spatula to turn the patties a quarter turn (don't flip) and cook for 3 more minutes until browned. Now, use a metal spatula to flip them onto their second side, place two slices of American cheese on top of each, and cook for an additional 3 to 4 minutes until the bottoms are browned and the cheese is melted. This will yield a rare to medium-rare burger—if you like yours medium, cook for an additional 3 to 4 minutes.

5. ASSEMBLE: Arrange the bun bottoms on a flat surface. Spoon some of the onion jam on each and top with one of the burgers. Top with some lettuce, drizzle with some Thousand Island, and add the top bun. Serve with pickles on the side.

BUN

DRESSING

LETTUCE

CHEESE

BURGER

ONION JAM

BUN

prep time: 20 minutes
(plus 20 minutes for chilling)
cook time: about 15 minutes
yield: 4 sandwiches

FRIED CHICKEN CUTLET SANDWICH
with sriracha mayo

This recipe is so Ava. The secret is to make sure the chicken is pounded really thinly so the sandwich is all about an even layer of each flavor from the bread to the spread. The chicken isn't preseasoned—instead, it's salted after it comes out of the pan—a real statement. Salt has a bigger impact when sprinkled over the crispy-hot breading, which, by the way, is made from two types of breadcrumbs, so it has that mix of more textured crispy shards from the panko and pleasantly sandy fine breadcrumbs on the exterior.

CHICKEN CUTLETS

2 large **eggs**

1½ cups **plain breadcrumbs**

1½ cups **panko breadcrumbs**

4 **chicken cutlets** (from the breast), 5 to 6 ounces each, pounded thin

¼ cup **olive oil**

Kosher salt

SRIRACHA MAYO

¼ cup **mayonnaise**

1 tablespoon **red wine vinegar**

2 teaspoons **garlic powder**

1 teaspoon **Sriracha**

SANDWICHES

1 medium head of **iceberg lettuce**, shredded

4 seeded **hamburger buns**

12 to 16 **pickle rounds**

1. Preheat the oven to 350°F. Line a plate with a paper towel.

2. PREPARE THE CHICKEN: In a medium bowl, whisk the eggs with a splash of cold water. In another medium bowl, combine the plain and panko breadcrumbs. Dip each cutlet thoroughly in the eggs and then through the breadcrumbs so both sides are well coated. Feel free to press the chicken into the breadcrumbs so they stick better on each side. Place the chicken in a single layer on a baking sheet and chill in the refrigerator for 20 minutes.

3. COOK THE CHICKEN: In a large skillet, heat the olive oil over medium heat. When the oil begins to smoke lightly, remove the pan from the heat and add the chicken pieces carefully in a single layer. Return the pan to the heat and cook on the first side until golden brown, 5 to 8 minutes. Use metal tongs or a large metal spatula to gently turn them on their second side. Cook for an additional 5 to 8 minutes until golden brown and firm to the touch. You can also use a meat thermometer inserted into the thickest part to check the doneness. The thermometer should register 165°F. Transfer the cutlets to the prepared plate to drain slightly. Season both sides of each cutlet with salt.

4. MAKE THE MAYO: In a medium bowl, whisk the mayonnaise, vinegar, garlic powder, and Sriracha. Taste for seasoning.

5. ASSEMBLE: Sprinkle some lettuce on the bottoms of the buns and top with some of the Sriracha mayo. (That way the lettuce protects the bread, and the mayo directly connects with and moistens the chicken cutlets.) Place a cutlet, more of the mayo, and the pickles on top. Top with the other half of the bread.

photographs on pages 80-81

prep time: 15 minutes (plus at
least 30 minutes for marinating)
cook time: 10 minutes
(plus 10 minutes for resting)
yield: 12 to 16 tacos

STEAK TACOS
with cabbage

I love this dish because, like my dad, I love steak. My mom loves to eat fish and vegetables mostly, but she can get on board when there are vegetables *around* the steak . . . and, well, we all love a taco (plus tacos are a great way to stretch a more expensive cut of meat like steak!). Be sure to use good-quality tortillas, made from pure corn or flour with no additives—you should be able to smell the corn or flour through the packaging, imho! A couple of tips about steak for tacos: Look at the meat; you will see all cuts have a natural grain, like wood. Once the steak is cooked and rested, slice against those lines for the tenderest bite. Resting the meat is annoying because it's hot and you want to eat it right away, but the truth is that the juices in the meat have to flow back through the meat once it's cooked to make it juicy throughout. It's worth the wait—if you slice the steak too soon, the juices will end up all over your cutting board instead (steak fail). Imagine the cabbage is like coleslaw on a deli sandwich or pickles on a burger. It's the juicy, vinegary factor that connects the meat and the tortilla.

CABBAGE	STEAK	TACOS
1 small head of **red cabbage**, cored	1 (2-pound) piece of **hanger steak**, trimmed of sinew	12 to 16 (6-inch) **corn tortillas**
2 tablespoons **red wine vinegar**	**Kosher salt**	1 large **avocado**, sliced or smashed, for serving
1 tablespoon **extra-virgin olive oil**	2 teaspoons **chili powder**	**Kosher salt**
1 teaspoon **Sriracha hot sauce**	2 tablespoons **canola oil**	Juice of 1 small **lime**
	1 tablespoon **balsamic vinegar**	

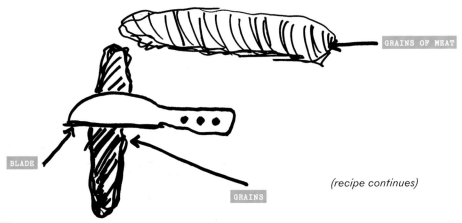

GRAINS OF MEAT

BLADE

GRAINS

(recipe continues)

1. MAKE THE CABBAGE: You can shred the cabbage in a food processor or, with some adult supervision, slice with a mandoline fitted with a safety guard. You can also place a half on a cutting board and thinly slice with a large kitchen knife. In a medium bowl, toss the cabbage with the red wine vinegar, olive oil, and Sriracha. Set aside for at least 30 minutes and up to 4 hours so the vinegar can work its magic.

2. COOK THE STEAK: Season the steak on all sides with salt. Use a small strainer to evenly dust the steak with the chili powder. Heat the oil in a large cast-iron skillet over medium heat. When the oil begins to smoke lightly, remove the pan from the heat and use a pair of tongs to gingerly place the steak in the hot oil. Return the pan to the heat and cook the meat over high heat until each side is browned, 3 to 4 minutes per side. Remove the steak from the heat and add the balsamic vinegar to the pan. Transfer the steak to a cutting board and allow it to rest for 10 minutes.

3. FINISH: Warm the tortillas, one by one, in a nonstick skillet over low heat, turning so both sides puff slightly and get lightly charred. Alternatively, char the tortillas (on both sides) over an open flame for a few seconds. This is a step that should definitely be done with a parent/adult present to monitor the heat and for safety. Peel, pit, and fork-crush the avocado. Season with salt and lime juice.

4. ASSEMBLE: Slice the steak, against the grain of the meat, into thin slices. Arrange some of the meat, avocado, and cabbage in an even line down the center of each tortilla. Remember that the best-tasting tacos are the ones that have all the different flavors of the filling in each bite. Serve immediately, folding the edges into the center to form a taco.

Mom Tip

If using a meat thermometer, rare registers between 125° to 130°F; for medium rare, 130° to 135°F; and between 135° to 140°F for medium. If you like your steak a little more cooked, leave it in the pan for a few minutes longer on each side, but note that tougher cuts like hanger, flank, and skirt like to be cooked on the rare side.

prep time: 15 minutes
cook time: 10 to 12 minutes
yield: 8 to 10 tacos

POBLANO + CHEESE TACOS

My mom and I eat this dish together almost every time we find ourselves at a Los Angeles taco joint. It's a shameless case of "I ate it in a few restaurants, so now I will make it at home in my own way." My mom doesn't take her inspiration from eating out in the same way I do. She marvels at the china plates, silverware, cocktails, napkins, and great service. I am far more fixated on the food, and when I find peppers and melted cheese wrapped in a little tortilla this satisfying, it becomes a part of my repertoire. My mom loves this dish, too—we bond over the charred peppers, which I turn into a zesty salsa—because my grandmother used to make a lot of roasted peppers and roasted tomatoes, and it reminds us of her (and we miss her). Get a jar of mild tomato salsa at the store to serve on the side. Sometimes I make some guacamole, too.

POBLANO SALSA

2 large **poblano peppers**

8 sprigs of **cilantro**, leaves removed from stems

1 small **garlic clove**, grated

1 tablespoon **red wine vinegar**

1 tablespoon **extra-virgin olive oil**

Kosher salt

TACOS

8 to 10 (6-inch) **corn tortillas**

1½ cups shredded **Monterey Jack cheese**

Store-bought mild **salsa**, for serving (optional)

1. Preheat the oven to 425°F.

2. MAKE THE SALSA: Place each poblano pepper directly on the flame of a burner set to low heat (if you don't have gas burners, use store-bought roasted peppers). Allow the skin of the pepper to char (turn black), using tongs to rotate it often, until all sides of the pepper are burned/blackened. Transfer the peppers to a plate and let them cool for a few minutes, then use a paper towel to wipe the charred skin off the pepper flesh. Remove the stem and seeds, open the pepper, and slice it into ¼-inch-wide strips. Add the peppers to a large bowl and mix with the cilantro, garlic, vinegar, and olive oil. Season with salt.

3. FINISH: Warm the tortillas, one by one, in a nonstick skillet over low heat, turning so both sides puff slightly and get lightly charred. Alternatively, char the tortillas (on both sides) over an open flame for a few seconds. This is a step that definitely should be done with a parent/adult present to monitor the heat and for safety.

4. ASSEMBLE: Arrange the tortillas in a single layer on two baking sheets and spoon some of the poblano salsa and cheese over each. Remember that the best-tasting tacos are ones that have all the different flavors of the fillings in each bite. Place the baking sheets in the oven and bake until the cheese melts, 3 to 5 minutes. Serve hot with the store-bought salsa on the side (if using).

photographs on pages 86–87

prep time: 10 minutes (plus at least 30 minutes for marinating)
cook time: none, unless making the ricotta (page 90)
yield: 6 to 8 servings

RICOTTA + TOMATO CROSTINI

I like to use more acidic, less expensive balsamic vinegar for this. Fancier aged balsamic (like the one from Giuseppe Giusti) is good when you want layered flavors—my mom would say "almost like a fine wine." This dish is heavy on the garlic and vinegar, which tastes so good with super ripe tomatoes. My mother always looks at me in surprise when I measure this recipe out—the extra vinegar (I know, it seems like a lot, but trust me!) is spooned over the crostini so it soaks into the bread and saturates it to the core, but the bread edges and surface remain crunchy as does the flaky salt—so tasty. If your ricotta has any extra liquid, drain the cheese on a kitchen towel or squeeze it in cheesecloth to remove excess before spooning it on the toast.

1 pint medium **cherry tomatoes**, halved

1 large ripe **beefsteak tomato**, coarsely diced

¼ cup **balsamic vinegar**

3 tablespoons **extra-virgin olive oil**

3 large **garlic cloves**, cut into thin slices

1 tablespoon **honey**

Maldon flaky sea salt

Freshly ground **black pepper**

1 (15-ounce) container **whole milk ricotta cheese** or homemade (recipe follows)

8 thick slices **sourdough bread**, toasted

½ cup finely grated **Parmesan cheese**

1. MARINATE THE TOMATOES: In a medium bowl, toss the cherry and beefsteak tomatoes with the balsamic, olive oil, garlic, honey, a generous pinch of salt, and some pepper. Marinate at room temperature for 30 minutes and up to 4 hours.

2. ASSEMBLE: Spread about 1 tablespoon of the ricotta over each slice of toasted bread and season with a pinch of salt. Spoon some of the tomato mix over the ricotta and finish with a generous sprinkle of Parmesan. Spoon extra vinegar from the bottom of the bowl onto the bread.

(recipe continues)

HOMEMADE RICOTTA

prep time: 5 minutes (plus at least 25 minutes for resting)
cook time: 10 minutes (plus a few hours for chilling)
yield: about 1 cup

If you're feeling experimental, make this version of homemade ricotta. Tasty!

1 cup **heavy cream**

½ cup **whole milk**

½ cup **full-fat buttermilk**

1. COOK: In a medium pot, bring the cream, milk, and buttermilk to a soft simmer over medium heat. Simmer gently for a few minutes, until the milk solids rise to the surface and form what looks like a raft. Turn off the heat and allow the milk to rest and cool on the stove, 25 to 30 minutes.

2. DRAIN: Line a strainer with a few layers of cheesecloth. Use a large slotted spoon to scoop the solids from the surface into the strainer. Pour the liquid gently over the solids in the strainer, allowing the liquid to flow through the strainer and trapping the solids in the cheesecloth. (The liquid is the whey and can be used to thicken soups or as a substitute for water in bread dough, among other things.)

3. Refrigerate the ricotta for a few hours to allow all the liquid to drain and so it firms up slightly. Transfer to an airtight container and store in the fridge for up to 2 weeks.

prep time: 10 minutes
cook time: none
yield: 4 to 6 servings

SMOKED SALMON TARTINE
with scallion cream cheese

This is like a classic New York deli moment you can create at home. I like dill so much that when I use it, I go all in. The simple combo of the salmon and the scallions with the tangy cream cheese and sourdough bread is just about perfect. When choosing the fish, I go for Scottish smoked salmon because the texture is slightly fatty and the flavor is "salmon-y" but not overly salty, which can be a turnoff to kids who often have a more sensitive palate than adults. If you can't find scallion cream cheese, simply slice 2 or 3 scallions and stir them into softened plain cream cheese. For best results, slice and toast the bread just as you are planning to assemble and eat. And to take this to the next level, finish with a spoonful of trout roe or salmon roe.

8 ounces (1 cup) **scallion cream cheese**, at room temperature

4 to 6 (½-inch-thick) slices **sourdough bread**, lightly toasted

Maldon flaky sea salt (optional)

½ pound thinly sliced **smoked salmon** (preferably Scottish)

Juice of ½ large **lemon**

Freshly ground **black pepper**

8 to 10 sprigs of **dill**, chopped, stems and all

Spread about 1 tablespoon of the cream cheese over each slice of bread and season with a pinch of salt (if using). Drape a slice or two of smoked salmon over the cream cheese. Top with a squeeze of lemon juice, a grind of pepper, and a generous sprinkling of dill.

Herbs and Stems

We make a lot of salsas and herb sauces at home, and for the "tender" herbs like dill, basil, cilantro, and flat-leaf parsley, we chop and add the stems in, too. Why waste them? The stems are tasty and often add a slightly juicy (and delicious) crunch. For wintry herbs like thyme, rosemary, and sage, we discard the stems because they are woody and often taste kind of like cough medicine.

SNACKS + HORS D'

Ava likes her "hors d'" and goes to great trouble to make them highly flavorful small bites. They are great when you have friends over or when you've had a long day and just want something snacky that also makes you feel special. In fact, Ava's hors d' are becoming more popular than mine at our little dinner parties. Some of these recipes are simply an assembly of tasty, familiar ingredients, while others require a batter or breading. Some require baking in the oven or even making a filling and assembling. You can move from the simplest in the beginning of the chapter to the harder ones deeper in. Or attack them in reverse—it's your call. Either way, you will challenge yourself and feel satisfied with the tasty results.

prep time: 10 minutes
(plus at least 2 hours for marinating)
cook time: none
yield: about 2 cups

AVA'S MARINATED CUCUMBERS

Everyone needs to know how to put together a few simple dishes, whether you're making them for a quick snack like I do, for a potluck at a friend's house, or for your future self's fancy office party years from now. These cucumbers are my go-to—they're easy to make but don't taste like anything ready-made or store-bought—not that there's anything wrong with that. In fact, this is the kind of snack that, when I make it, my mom looks at me like I'm from another planet because when *she* was my age, she would've reached for a few olives, pickles, or something else ready-made. Anyways . . . it's the combo of crunchy cukes with the zing of red pepper flakes and fish sauce paired with the mellow vinegar and the touch of sweetness from the honey that makes you keep eating them! Don't like spicy? Omit the pepper flakes. Don't like funky? Omit the fish sauce. Eat them as is or put them on burgers and sandwiches, in quesadillas, or even on a cheese board.

2 tablespoons **Maldon flaky sea salt**

2 tablespoons **white sesame seeds**

4 large **garlic cloves**, thinly sliced crosswise

¾ cup **rice wine vinegar**

2 tablespoons **honey**

1 tablespoon **fish sauce**

¼ teaspoon **dried red pepper flakes**

2 **English cucumbers**, peeled, or 8 **Persian cucumbers**, unpeeled, cut into ½-inch rounds

In a large bowl, combine the salt, sesame seeds, and garlic with the vinegar, honey, fish sauce, and red pepper flakes. Taste for seasoning, add the cucumbers, and transfer to an airtight container. Marinate for at least 2 hours and up to 3 days before serving. Store in an airtight container in the fridge for up to 2 weeks.

Mom Tip

English cucumbers are big, hearty, and surprisingly savory. Smaller Persian cucumbers are sweet and crunchy. Ava loves using them both, in combination.

prep time: 10 to 15 minutes
cook time: none
yield: 8 to 10 stuffed celery sticks
and 1 cup sauce

TZATZIKI "ANTS ON A LOG"

Tzatziki is a Greek sauce (and dip) that is made super delicious with the addition of grated cucumbers. The cukes bring on a succulent, juicy quality that is so great when stuffed into juicy celery—and are a big way to level up one of my favorite after-school snacks: ants on a log. I love the crunch of the celery against the creaminess of the yogurt with the freshness of the dill (and because I'm a freak for dill, sometimes I double the amount of it). The golden raisin "ants" add tang and sweetness to the celery "log." You can also use sweeter brown raisins or even cut-up dried apricots, too. I do think it's important to serve the tzatziki stuffed into chilled celery straight out of the fridge. You can also use halved carrots in place of the celery.

TZATZIKI SAUCE

1 large **English cucumber**

1 large **garlic clove**, grated

Kosher salt

Freshly ground **black pepper**

1½ cups **full-fat plain Greek yogurt**

2 tablespoons **extra-virgin olive oil**

1 tablespoon **red wine vinegar**

4 sprigs of **dill**, coarsely chopped

1 medium **lemon**

LOGS

8 to 10 **celery stalks**, peeled with a vegetable peeler

¼ cup **golden raisins**

Sea salt

1. PREPARE THE CUCUMBERS: Using a box grater, grate the cucumber on the largest set of holes into a large bowl. Transfer to a strainer to drain the cucumbers and then place them in the center of a clean, sturdy kitchen towel. Twist the towel up and wring out all the excess water (do this over the sink!).

2. MAKE THE TZATZIKI: Transfer the grated cucumbers to a large bowl (ideally, you'll have about 1½ cups) and stir in the garlic, a generous pinch of kosher salt and grind of pepper, the yogurt, olive oil, vinegar, and dill. Lightly zest the lemon five or six times into the bowl. Halve the lemon, juice it, and add all the juice. Stir and taste for seasoning.

3. ASSEMBLE: Spread the tzatziki in the wells of the celery and top each log with a few golden raisins. Sprinkle with a little sea salt and serve.

Peeling Celery? Why?

Celery is delicious unpeeled, sure. But when you remove that outer skin, the texture becomes smoother, and the natural sweetness of the celery is far more pronounced. Peel the celery in long, even strokes using a square peeler, if you have one. No need to peel the inside, just the rounded exterior. It's an extra step that elevates a staple vegetable we have been eating all our lives. Try it.

prep time: 25 minutes
(plus at least 2 hours for chilling)
cook time: 35 to 40 minutes
yield: 18 mozzarella sticks

MOZZARELLA STICKS
with tomato dipping sauce

These never get old, especially to me. I love them right out of the oven while they're hot and oozy . . . and making them from scratch is so satisfying and actually pretty easy. I sometimes prep a batch and just bake off a few here and there as a snack (they keep well in the fridge for up to 2 days or freeze for a couple of weeks). You can use jarred tomato sauce to save time and just make the mozzarella sticks from scratch. I have tried a lot of fancy types of mozzarella with this recipe and find that the string cheese kind is most likely to survive the cooking process. You're gonna want to fry them right away, but believe me when I say, patience is key—it's important for them to chill for at least 2 hours so the breading sticks better.

TOMATO SAUCE

3 tablespoons **extra-virgin olive oil**

4 large **garlic cloves**, grated

Kosher salt

2 tablespoons **tomato paste**

1 (14.5-ounce) can **whole peeled tomatoes**

2 teaspoons **sugar**

½ cup **heavy cream**

Leaves from 2 sprigs of **basil**

MOZZARELLA STICKS

4 large **eggs**

1 to 1½ cups **panko breadcrumbs**

1 cup finely grated **Parmesan cheese**

2 tablespoons **dried oregano**

18 **mozzarella string cheese sticks**

1 quart (4 cups) **canola oil**, for frying

Kosher salt

1 to 2 tablespoons **garlic powder**

(recipe continues)

1. MAKE THE SAUCE: In a large skillet, warm the olive oil and garlic over medium heat until fragrant, about 2 minutes. Add a pinch of salt and 2 tablespoons water. Simmer until the water cooks out and the garlic becomes tender, 2 to 3 minutes. Stir in the tomato paste with 2 more tablespoons water and cook to fry the paste for a minute in the oil, stirring until it starts to sizzle and break apart. Add the whole tomatoes and sugar and cook over medium heat, 12 to 15 minutes, until the tomatoes soften. Stir in the cream. Season with salt to taste. Puree in a blender until smooth and keep warm.

2. MAKE THE STICKS: Line a baking sheet with parchment paper. Add the eggs to a large bowl and lightly whisk to combine. In another large bowl, mix together the breadcrumbs with ¾ cup of the Parmesan and the oregano. Dip a mozzarella stick in the egg, turning it to coat, and place in the breadcrumbs, rolling to coat. Repeat, dipping again in the egg and rolling through the breadcrumbs. Arrange the sticks on the prepared baking sheet and repeat with the remaining sticks. Refrigerate for at least 2 hours and up to 12 hours.

3. Preheat the oven to 300°F. Place a baking sheet in the oven.

4. FRY: Pour the oil into a deep heavy-bottomed pot. Heat the oil over medium heat until it reaches 350°F on an instant-read thermometer. Set a wire rack over another baking sheet. Drop about six of the sticks into the oil and fry until they are browned, 3 to 4 minutes, then use a slotted spoon to transfer them, one at a time, to the rack. Ask an adult for help here if you need it! Season each stick immediately with salt and garlic powder. Place on the baking sheet in the oven to keep warm while you fry more (if you are frying more).

5. SERVE: Spoon the tomato sauce into a side bowl. Tear the basil leaves and stir them into the sauce. Arrange the mozzarella sticks on a platter, sprinkle with the remaining ¼ cup Parmesan, and serve immediately.

prep time: 10 minutes (plus resting time)
cook time: 4 to 6 minutes per batch
yield: 8 to 10 large pancakes or
16 to 18 smaller ones

KIMCHI PANCAKES

My mom says kimchi—the spicy, tangy fermented cabbage that is a must in most Korean households—is succulent. I say it's juicy. She says it has a great salinity. I say it has an addictive saltiness that makes you keep eating. It's just funky fermented cabbage that has a bit of heat to it, but I can't resist grabbing a jar at the supermarket (it never lasts long in our house). This pancake batter is also great without the kimchi and with a cup of sliced scallions added instead. To serve, I literally just put the pancakes on a plate with some soy sauce for dunking and watch them disappear. (If you're sensitive to heat, you can rinse off some of the spice from the cabbage before chopping it up.)

2 cups **all-purpose flour**

½ cup **cornstarch**

2 teaspoons **baking powder**

2 cups **club soda**

1 large **egg yolk**

1 cup **kimchi**, drained and coarsely chopped, plus extra for serving

¼ to ⅓ cup **canola oil**, for frying

Low-sodium **soy sauce**, for serving (optional)

1. Preheat the oven to 300°F. Place a baking sheet in the oven.

2. MAKE THE BATTER: In a large bowl, whisk together the flour, cornstarch, and baking powder. Whisk in the club soda and egg yolk, stirring just until no dry streaks remain (do not overmix or the batter will yield tough pancakes). Let the batter rest for 15 minutes in the refrigerator.

3. MAKE THE PANCAKES: Stir the kimchi into the batter. Heat a large nonstick skillet and add about 1 tablespoon of the oil. When it gets hot and smokes lightly, add spoonfuls of the batter—about 4 tablespoons for a large pancake and 2 tablespoons for smaller ones—leaving space between each to spread as they cook. Cook for 2 to 3 minutes or until brown on the first side. Use a spatula to flip each on its second side and cook for an additional 2 to 3 minutes. Obviously, the cooking time will be a little longer if your pancakes are bigger in size. Transfer to the baking sheet in the oven to keep warm while you repeat with the remaining batter.

4. SERVE: Arrange the pancakes on a serving platter with soy sauce on the side for dunking (if using) and more kimchi.

prep time: 15 minutes
cook time: 20 minutes
yield: 4 to 6 servings

BAKED CHICKEN WINGS
with garlicky ranch

I'm all about ranch dressing with my wings, while my mom is a traditionalist and goes for blue cheese—sometimes I'll make a small batch of blue cheese just for her so she doesn't have fomo. To my beloved ranch, I add tons of garlic powder and anchovies. There is such bias against anchovies—I don't get it. If you like umami, you like anchovies, full stop. So, let's keep it moving! I know the nonstick spray move with the chicken is odd, but it prevents sticking (duh) and actually keeps the chicken wings from getting too greasy (cool!) in the oven. This is an anytime meal for me—I even eat these wings for breakfast (protein for breakfast that's not in the form of bacon or sausage is a *thing* . . . try it). For the hot sauce, you can leave it out if you don't like spicy—I promise not to judge. I like Frank's RedHot or Crystal hot sauce mixed with a tiny splash of Tabasco. I guess, like my mom, I'm a bit of a traditionalist.

RANCH DRESSING

1 cup (8 ounces) **sour cream**

½ cup **mayonnaise**

½ cup **full-fat buttermilk**

4 **anchovy fillets**, finely chopped, plus 1 tablespoon of oil from the tin

1 small **garlic clove**, grated

1 tablespoon **Worcestershire sauce**

1 tablespoon **hot sauce**

2 teaspoons **red wine vinegar**

2 teaspoons **garlic powder**

2 teaspoons **kosher salt**

6 sprigs of **dill**, chopped, stems and all

WINGS

½ stick (4 tablespoons) **unsalted butter**

2 tablespoons **hot sauce**

12 **chicken wings** (about 2 pounds)

Nonstick cooking spray

Kosher salt

(recipe continues)

1. MAKE THE DRESSING: In a large bowl, whisk together the sour cream, mayonnaise, and buttermilk with the anchovies and their oil, grated garlic, Worcestershire, hot sauce, vinegar, garlic powder, salt, and dill. Taste for seasoning.

2. MAKE THE SAUCE: In a medium pot, add the butter and hot sauce and cook over medium-low heat to gently melt the butter, stirring to combine. Leave the pot on the stove to keep warm.

3. Preheat the oven to 450°F.

4. GET READY: Set the wings on a cutting board. Cut between the drumstick ("drum") piece and the flatter second ("flat") piece to separate. (Freeze the wing tips in a resealable plastic bag for making chicken stock.) Use paper towels to dry the chicken wings of any excess moisture. Line a baking sheet with parchment paper and lightly coat with nonstick spray. Arrange the drums and flats on top, leaving space between each so they can brown when they cook. Season with a generous, even sprinkling of salt.

5. BAKE: Place the baking sheet in the center of the oven and bake until the chicken wings are crisp and bubbling, 18 to 20 minutes.

6. FINISH: Use metal tongs or a slotted spoon to transfer the wings to a large bowl. Drizzle the sauce over the chicken and toss to combine. Serve with the ranch dressing on the side.

prep time: 15 to 20 minutes
cook time: 20 to 25 minutes
yield: 8 skewers
equipment: 8 thick, sturdy
wooden (soak in water 20 minutes
prior to grilling) or metal skewers

TSUKUNE
with yakitori sauce

JAPANESE CHICKEN MEATBALL SKEWERS

These chicken skewers are to die for. There's the silky texture of the chicken, and the deep, almost meaty taste of the yakitori sauce, *and* it's on a skewer. They're inspired by one of my favorite Japanese restaurants—I've been eating their meatball skewers for years. Grilling gives the meat an incredibly smoky, charcoal flavor that is so good with the sweet-salty yakitori sauce (imho, the sauce makes the dish). My mom taught me to nearly fully cook the meatballs in water and then brown and glaze them on the grill so they don't dry out or get overly charred—good tip! If you don't have a grill or grill pan you can finish cooking the meatballs in a sauté pan with a little hot oil until they are cooked through.

1 pound ground
chicken breast

1 cup **panko breadcrumbs**

1 small **shallot**,
grated on a Microplane

2 teaspoons finely grated
ginger

1 tablespoon, plus 1½ teaspoons
cornstarch

Kosher salt

1 large **egg**, lightly beaten

4 tablespoons
low-sodium **soy sauce**

3 tablespoons **mirin rice wine**

2 tablespoons
rice wine vinegar

1 tablespoon **sugar**

2 to 3 tablespoons **canola oil**

1. MAKE THE MEATBALLS: In a large bowl, combine the chicken with the breadcrumbs, shallot, ginger, cornstarch, a generous sprinkle of salt, the egg, and 2 tablespoons of the soy sauce. Use a rubber spatula to combine and then add the vinegar. Roll the mixture into 24 meatballs (or 18 to 20 cylinders).

2. Set a wire rack over a baking sheet. Fill a shallow 2-quart pot three-quarters full with water and bring it to a simmer over medium heat. Season the water with salt. Rub a wooden spoon with oil (to prevent the meatballs from sticking and splashing the water) and carefully drop in 6 to 8 meatballs. Simmer until they are completely cooked through, 5 to 7 minutes (test one by removing it and cutting it in half). Use a slotted spoon to transfer them to the rack. Return the water to a simmer and repeat with the remaining meatballs.

3. MAKE THE SAUCE: While the meatballs are cooling, in a small saucepan, combine the remaining 2 tablespoons soy sauce, mirin, vinegar, and sugar and cook over medium heat until slightly thick, 2 to 3 minutes.

4. Preheat a grill or a grill pan. While it's heating, thread three meatballs (or 1 cylinder) on the upper half of each skewer.

5. GRILL AND GLAZE: Get an adult for this part! When the grill starts to smoke, dip a kitchen towel in the oil and use it to grease the grill grates. Arrange a few skewers side by side. Cook for 5 to 7 minutes until browned, grill marked, and hot. Repeat with the remaining skewers. Using a brush, glaze the meatballs with the sauce and serve warm.

prep time: 30 to 35 minutes
(plus at least 2 hours for marinating)
cook time: 25 minutes
yield: about 30 dumplings

PORK DUMPLINGS

There is something so satisfying about making my own dumplings or raviolis. It makes me feel like I can do anything. Making my own filling is also a great way to get a sense of how to season ground meats—my mom taught me to season the filling and then cook a little in a skillet so I can taste it to make sure the flavors are on point. You can make dumpling dough easily from scratch, but store-bought wrappers are just as good and will keep for a long time in the freezer.

DUMPLINGS

Kosher salt

½ teaspoon **baking soda**

4 **baby bok choy** (or 1 large), ends discarded and leaves and stalks thinly sliced

1 pound ground **pork**

6 **scallions** (white and green parts), thinly sliced

1 tablespoon finely grated **ginger**

1 large **egg**, lightly beaten

2 tablespoons **cornstarch**

1 tablespoon **mirin rice wine**

2 teaspoons low-sodium **soy sauce**

1. COOK THE BOK CHOY: Bring a large pot of water to a boil. Season the water with salt (it should taste like mild seawater), then add the baking soda. Prepare an ice bath by filling a bowl large enough to hold the bok choy with ice and cold water. Add the bok choy to the boiling water and cook until the color of the leaves brightens and the stalks are crisp-tender, 2 to 3 minutes. Use a slotted spoon to transfer them immediately to the ice bath. Allow them to sit for a few minutes, swirling them gently in the water until they are fully cooled (they'll crisp up a bit, too). Transfer the bok choy to a clean kitchen towel spread on a flat surface. Thoroughly pat dry and finely chop.

2. MAKE THE FILLING: Gently spread the pork across the bottom and up the sides of a large bowl. Sprinkle the meat with the scallions, ginger, and egg. In a small bowl, stir the cornstarch, mirin, and soy sauce together until smooth. Sprinkle the soy sauce mixture over the meat, add the bok choy, and mix everything together until just combined—don't overmix. Refrigerate for at least 2 hours and ideally overnight, so the flavors can meld together.

3. MAKE THE DIPPING SAUCE: In a medium bowl, combine the ginger and garlic with the soy sauce, vinegar, sesame oil, and sesame seeds and whisk with 2 tablespoons water. Taste for seasoning.

DIPPING SAUCE

1 tablespoon
finely grated **ginger**

2 medium **garlic cloves**,
grated

3 tablespoons low-sodium
soy sauce

2 tablespoons
red wine vinegar

2 teaspoons **sesame oil**

1 tablespoon
white sesame seeds

30 round **dumpling wrappers**

2 tablespoons **canola oil**

4. FILL AND FORM: Line a baking sheet with parchment paper. Arrange a few dumpling wrappers at a time on a flat surface. Place a scant tablespoon of filling in the center of each, wet the edges of each wrapper with water, and close them like a half moon, pressing the edges together. Fold four to six "pleats" in the edges of each dumpling. Repeat with the remaining wrappers and filling and arrange the dumplings in a single layer on the prepared baking sheet. Refrigerate until ready to cook.

5. COOK THE DUMPLINGS: Heat a large skillet over medium heat and add 1 tablespoon of the canola oil. Arrange half of the dumplings in a single layer and let them brown for 2 to 3 minutes. Use metal tongs to turn them over, then add about ⅓ cup water to the pan, tightly cover, and steam the dumplings until cooked through, 5 to 7 minutes. They should look translucent when cooked. Transfer to a serving platter. Repeat with the remaining oil and dumplings. Serve with the dipping sauce. You can premake a batch of these and freeze them in a resealable plastic bag for up to 2 months. When ready to eat, thaw them for about 15 minutes to take the chill off and cook as instructed.

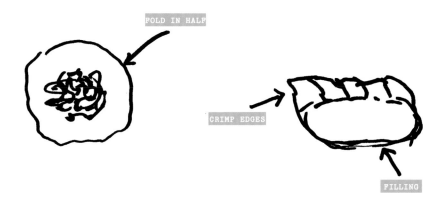

FOLD IN HALF

CRIMP EDGES

FILLING

photographs on pages 112-113

PASTAS

Here, the simplest pastas, like the buttered noodles, start the chapter, and then you slowly progress to bolder flavors and ingredients. The sauces are easy, and the pasta types are super fun. The sauces can mostly be made in advance, and the pasta just cooked, tossed with sauce, and served. (Some of the dishes can be made totally in advance, like the stuffed shells on page 125). The thing about pasta dishes is that they are great eaten hot right out of the pan, or cold standing at the open fridge door. They are often tastier a day or two after they are made, and best of all, they never go out of style. People always want a red-sauce-joint vibe at home . . . and here's how to do it.

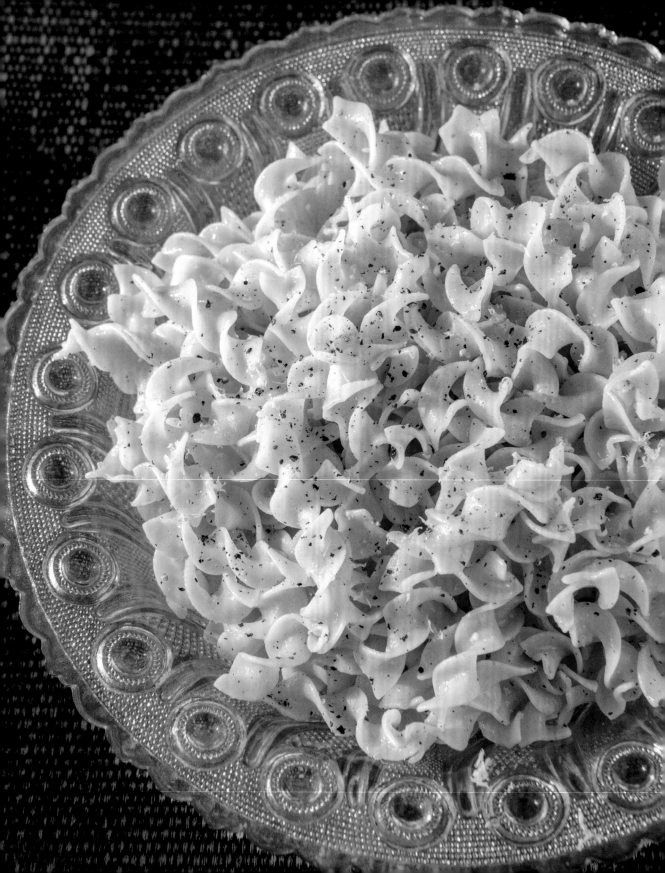

prep time: 5 minutes
cook time: 6 to 7 minutes
yield: 4 to 6 servings

TEN-MINUTE BUTTERY EGG NOODLES

This is the simplest recipe for pasta, and the one that every cook (kids *and* adults!) should have in their back pocket—this is starter pasta at its finest. Did you know that ordinary noodles are made from a basic wheat, whereas pasta is made from semolina flour? Semolina is a lot coarser than all-purpose flour, which enhances the texture of the pasta. I began eating this dish at an age when I didn't yet know the taste of a caper or an anchovy. Simple buttered noodles are a great place to begin exploring your own taste preferences—like adding a squeeze of lemon and some black pepper or maybe some fried capers.

1 pound dry **egg noodles** or a classic dry, eggy pasta such as fettuccine

Kosher salt

¾ stick (6 tablespoons) **unsalted butter**, thinly sliced

1 large **garlic clove**, grated

Zest and juice of 1 small **lemon**

Freshly ground **black pepper**

1. COOK THE NOODLES: Bring a large pot of water to a rolling boil. Season the water with salt (it should taste like mild seawater). Add the noodles to the pot and stir so they don't stick to the bottom as they cook. Cook the pasta until al dente, chewy but not hard or raw tasting, 6 to 7 minutes, or follow the package instructions. Reserve about ½ cup pasta water and drain the pasta in a colander.

2. MAKE THE SAUCE: While the noodles are cooking, combine the butter, garlic, and lemon zest in a large bowl.

3. FINISH: Add the hot pasta and reserved pasta water to the bowl with the other ingredients and toss vigorously with two large spoons to coat the pasta. The butter will melt and will link up with the pasta water to create the simplest coating for the pasta. Season with pepper and a tiny squeeze of lemon juice. Taste for seasoning and serve.

Mom Tip

Dress up even the simplest dish by serving it on a sophisticated plate. It's like wearing fancy jewelry with comfy sweatpants.

prep time: 10 minutes
cook time: 15 to 20 minutes
(mostly inactive)
yield: 4 to 6 servings

AGLIO E OLIO FROM THE MOVIE *CHEF*

This pasta is honestly otherworldly. It's the simplest pasta recipe ever—and that's what makes it so special. As the garlic sautés, it infuses the olive oil—that flavor combined with the parsley and lemon is just *really* good. I saw this recipe being made in a movie my mom and I really like called *Chef.* Most people might watch that movie and walk away craving kettle corn or a Cubano sandwich. For me, it was all about that pasta dish. In this one scene, Jon Favreau cooks this pasta for Scarlett Johansson—and I swear you can see that she tastes all the emotion he poured into the food. I love to imagine that we do that as home cooks, too—combine ingredients with such thoughtfulness. That scene always makes me so hungry and inspires me to cook! Pecorino cheese is slightly saltier than Parmesan—I love that extra saltiness in this dish. It's "salty" like the chef in the movie and even like my mom. Ha ha.

¼ cup **extra-virgin olive oil**

12 large **garlic cloves**, thinly sliced

Kosher salt

½ teaspoon **dried red pepper flakes**

12 sprigs of **flat-leaf parsley**, chopped, stems and all

Juice of 1 large **lemon**

1 pound **spaghetti**

1 small block of **Pecorino cheese**

1. MAKE THE SAUCE: Set a medium saucepan over medium-low heat (if the pan is smoking hot, the garlic will burn). Pour in the olive oil and once you see ripples forming in the oil, add the garlic and sauté with a pinch of salt and the red pepper flakes. Cook for 8 minutes, stirring from time to time, and then kill the heat. Stir the parsley into the garlic and oil—the residual heat will finish the cooking without burning anything. Add the lemon juice.

2. COOK THE PASTA: Bring a large pot of water to a rolling boil. Season the water with salt (it should taste like mild seawater), add the spaghetti, and cook, stirring with a slotted spoon to make sure the pasta doesn't clump or stick to the bottom as it cooks, until tender but still chewy, or al dente, 5 to 8 minutes. Set 1 cup of pasta water aside, then drain the pasta in a large colander.

3. ASSEMBLE AND SERVE: Transfer the pasta into the sauce. If the sauce looks too thick, loosen with some of the pasta water, adding a little at a time, and toss with tongs or a large metal spoon until you have the consistency you want (I like mine well combined but loose enough to enjoy the pasta mixing with the sauce). Grate the cheese over top.

PARSLEY

GARLIC   PASTA

TWIRL YOUR PASTA HIGH!!!

prep time: 15 minutes
cook time: 25 to 30 minutes
yield: 4 to 6 servings

GNOCCHI MACARONI + CHEESE

While this is my mom's recipe, it's practically straight from the kitchen of Butter restaurant, where I spent some time after school, working in various areas of the kitchen. I'd make little salads and other simple dishes and bring them to the chef, Michael Jenkins, for him to taste and give feedback. I rolled buttery Parker House rolls with pastry chef Kevin O'Brien. I cleaned fish fillets with Jamaal Dunlap. No matter who I was learning from, there was one constant every time: a pan of this gnocchi bubbling on the stove. It's irresistible and goes with anything from a salad to a giant steak to roasted vegetables. To me, it's one of the ultimate comfort foods. If you prefer, you could toss the sauce with cooked elbow macaroni instead of gnocchi to make mac and cheese.

3 cups **heavy cream**

2 tablespoons **Dijon mustard**

3½ cups finely grated **Gruyère cheese**

Kosher salt

Freshly ground **black pepper**

1 cup finely grated **Parmesan cheese**

1 teaspoon **Worcestershire sauce**

1 teaspoon **Tabasco**

1 large **garlic clove**, grated

1 pound **potato gnocchi**

2 tablespoons **unsalted butter**, melted

½ cup **panko breadcrumbs**

1. Preheat the oven to 350°F.

2. MAKE THE SAUCE: In a large pot, bring the cream to a simmer over medium heat. Use a wooden spoon to gently stir in the mustard and 3 cups of the Gruyère. Season with a pinch of salt and a few turns of pepper. Simmer gently, stirring constantly, until the cheese is melted and integrates with the cream. Add ½ cup of the Parmesan, the Worcestershire, Tabasco, and garlic. Taste for seasoning.

3. COOK THE GNOCCHI: In a large pot, bring 1 quart (4 cups) water to a rolling boil over medium-high heat. Season the water with salt (it should taste like mild seawater).

4. Add the gnocchi and stir with a wooden spoon or a large slotted spoon to ensure they do not stick to the bottom of the pot as they cook. Cook for 6 to 8 minutes or until the gnocchi float to the surface of the water, appearing tender and slightly puffed. Drain in a colander.

5. FINISH: Add the gnocchi to the cream sauce and stir gently to blend. Let them rest on the stove for 5 to 10 minutes so they absorb the flavors of the sauce. Stir in the remaining ½ cup Gruyère. In a medium bowl, mix the butter and breadcrumbs. Season with a pinch of salt and the remaining ½ cup Parmesan. Transfer the gnocchi to an oven-safe 8 x 11-inch baking dish and top with the seasoned breadcrumbs. Place the dish in the center of the oven and bake for 10 to 15 minutes or until hot and bubbling. Serve immediately.

prep time: 15 to 20 minutes
cook time: 45 to 50 minutes (mostly inactive)
yield: 4 to 6 servings

TURKEY BOLOGNESE

This is something my mom makes from time to time. It's kind of weird because I know she grew up eating only Bolognese made with beef. Now she makes it with turkey, which she says makes it lighter without losing the essence of the dish. This feels like a very American version of an Italian dish to me—which isn't a bad thing (that said, I'm sure my grandmother would only approve of beef for the Bolognese!). The milk she stirs in at the end is a classic touch that adds a little sweetness that mellows the tomatoes in the sauce. That's a traditional finish to a Bolognese sauce. It's almost as if the milk is a naturally sweet nod to a classic cream sauce without the heaviness.

5 tablespoons
extra-virgin olive oil

2 ounces **pancetta**,
finely chopped

1 medium **carrot**, grated

2 **celery stalks**, thinly sliced

1 medium **shallot**,
halved and thinly sliced

5 **garlic cloves**, minced

1 teaspoon **sugar**

Kosher salt

1 (28-ounce) can **whole peeled
tomatoes** with their juices

1½ pounds ground **turkey**
(preferably dark meat)

¼ teaspoon
dried red pepper flakes

¼ cup **whole milk**

1 pound **penne pasta**

1 cup finely grated
Parmesan cheese

1. MAKE THE SAUCE: In a medium skillet, heat 2 tablespoons of the olive oil over medium heat. Add the pancetta and cook for 1 minute, stirring so it browns and crisps slightly. Add the carrot, celery, shallot, and garlic. Season with the sugar and a generous pinch of salt and cook, stirring from time to time, for 5 to 8 minutes or until the shallots become translucent. Add the tomatoes and their juices and simmer over low heat, breaking up the tomatoes with a wooden spoon in the pot, for 12 to 15 minutes.

2. COOK THE TURKEY: Heat a large skillet over medium-high heat and add the remaining 3 tablespoons olive oil. When the oil begins to smoke lightly, remove the pan from the heat and add the ground turkey in a single layer. Return the pan to the heat, season with a generous pinch of salt, add the red pepper flakes, and brown the meat over medium heat without stirring, 3 to 5 minutes. Cook for another 5 to 8 minutes, stirring occasionally, or until the meat is no longer translucent and is cooked through like a hamburger. Taste for seasoning. Pour the tomato sauce and the milk over the turkey and stir to blend. Simmer over medium heat for 2 to 3 minutes, then turn off the heat and allow the sauce to rest while you cook the pasta.

3. COOK THE PASTA: Bring a large pot of water to a rolling boil. Season the water with salt (it should taste like mild seawater). Add the penne, stirring with a slotted spoon to make sure it doesn't clump or stick to the bottom of the pot as it cooks, and cook until tender but still chewy, or al dente, 5 to 8 minutes. Drain the pasta in a large colander, reserving ½ cup of the pasta water in case you need it to adjust the flavors and thickness of your sauce.

4. SERVE: Add the pasta to the skillet with the Bolognese and use a large metal spoon or tongs to toss to combine. If it's too thick, loosen the sauce with some of the pasta water—ideally, the sauce will coat the pasta well without being too thick or too runny. Top with the Parmesan and serve.

Pasta Cooking Water

What's the big deal? It's just spaghetti water, right? Well, as the pasta boils, starches are released into the cooking water—the water then becomes almost an ingredient in itself, since the thick-ish water can now be used to help loosen an overly thick sauce or even make a sauce in and of itself when added to some grated cheese or butter. Always save some in case you want to adjust your dish in the last moments or the pasta cools and clumps. Hot pasta water can fix that.

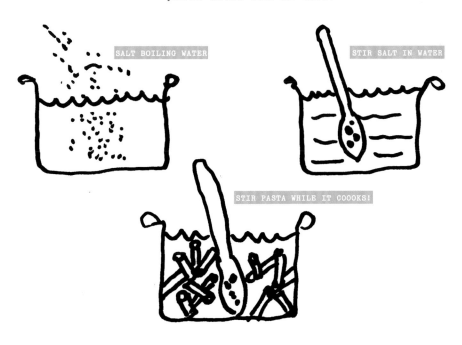

SALT BOILING WATER

STIR SALT IN WATER

STIR PASTA WHILE IT COOOKS!

prep time: 20 minutes
cook time: 30 to 40 minutes
(plus resting time)
yield: 4 to 6 servings

RICOTTA-STUFFED SHELLS

This is a dish my mother, Ava's grandma, used to make, and Ava just picked it up and made it a part of our repertoire. The shells are such an old-school form of pasta—when you're a kid, they're kind of like a precursor to ravioli. The acid of the tomatoes and the creaminess of the ricotta work together to bring this dish to life. Ava sometimes likes to drizzle olive oil over a few ½-inch-thick eggplant rounds, sprinkle them with salt, and bake them on a baking sheet lined with parchment paper alongside the shells. She serves them like a stack of pancakes on the side (and, like a substitute for sausages or meatballs with the shells—my mom would've loved this smart swap). Broccolini would work well here, too.

Kosher salt

1 pound large **pasta shells**

2 cups **whole milk ricotta cheese** (store-bought or homemade, page 90)

¾ cup finely grated **Parmesan cheese**, plus more for serving

¼ teaspoon **nutmeg** (preferably freshly grated)

1 large **egg**, lightly beaten

6 sprigs of **basil**, chopped, stems and all

3 cups **tomato sauce**, store-bought or homemade

1. COOK THE PASTA: Bring a large pot of water to a rolling boil. Season the water with salt (it should taste like mild seawater). Add the shells and stir with a large slotted spoon to ensure the pasta does not stick to the pan (or to itself) as it cooks. Cook until still quite firm, 6 to 8 minutes. Drain and refrigerate on a baking sheet.

2. Preheat the oven to 375°F.

3. PREPARE THE RICOTTA FILLING: Gently spread the ricotta across the bottom and up the sides of a large bowl. Season with salt and sprinkle half of the Parmesan over it in an even layer. Use a small strainer to sift the nutmeg in an even layer over the cheese. Add the egg and basil and mix to blend.

4. STUFF AND BAKE: Spread a little sauce across the bottom of a 13 x 9-inch baking dish. Remove the shells from the fridge and spoon about 1 tablespoon of the filling into each shell. Arrange the shells snugly in a single layer in the dish. Spoon the remaining sauce over the shells and place the dish in the oven. Bake until browned and the cheese is crisp around the edges, 15 to 18 minutes. Top with the remaining Parmesan and place the dish under the broiler for 2 to 3 minutes to finish. Let the shells rest for 10 to 15 minutes to settle. Taste for seasoning and serve with more Parmesan.

photographs on pages 126–127

Mix Off the Wall

Why spread the ricotta around the sides of the bowl? That way you can season it evenly and quickly instead of dropping the seasoning all in one place and stirring it more—which often leads to a tougher texture. The minute salt hits the wet ricotta, it dissolves all in one place. Better to sprinkle it all around! This is true for meatballs, too—and on page 110, you'll see we use the same mixing method as we call out here.

prep time: 10 minutes
cook time: 35 minutes
yield: 6 to 8 servings

PENNE ALLA VODKA

This is a red-sauce-joint type of dish, and honestly, it's maybe not your first thought of the kind of pasta you want to make if you're a kid. Its richness and pinky-red sauce comes from the cream and vodka that together work to balance the acidity of the tomatoes so nicely. Yes, there is vodka in the sauce—its purpose is to be a bridge between the creamy and tomatoey flavors in the sauce—but don't stress about it—the alcohol gets almost fully cooked out in the dish before serving. If using vodka, go for the cheap stuff because its edginess gets buried by other strong flavors—there's no reason to use expensive vodka here. If you're not comfortable using vodka, simply omit it and add a splash of rice wine in its place.

2 tablespoons **extra-virgin olive oil**

1 medium **yellow onion**, finely chopped

2 large **garlic cloves**, minced

Kosher salt

¼ cup **cheapo vodka**

2 teaspoons **sugar**

¼ teaspoon **dried red pepper flakes**

1 (14.5-ounce) can **whole peeled tomatoes** and their juices

¼ cup **heavy cream**, at room temperature

1 pound **penne pasta**

½ cup finely grated **Parmesan cheese**

1. MAKE THE SAUCE: In a large skillet, heat the olive oil over medium heat. Add the onion and garlic and season with salt. Stir in the vodka, sugar, and red pepper flakes. Cook the vodka down for about 5 minutes until the mixture has almost no liquid, then add the tomatoes. (If you add the tomatoes too soon and the vodka hasn't cooked out, there could be an unpleasant raw alcohol flavor in your sauce, so don't rush this step.) Turn the heat to medium-low and simmer for an additional 12 to 15 minutes, stirring from time to time and breaking the tomatoes up with a wooden spoon as they soften. Cook until the tomatoes taste cooked—there should be no canned tomato taste. Taste for seasoning, then stir in the cream. Transfer to a blender and puree until smooth. Keep warm.

2. COOK THE PASTA: Bring a large pot of water to a rolling boil. Season the water with salt (it should taste like mild seawater), add the penne, and cook, stirring with a slotted spoon to make sure the pasta doesn't clump or stick to the bottom as it cooks, until tender but still chewy, or al dente. Set ½ cup of the pasta water aside, then drain the pasta in a large colander.

3. ASSEMBLE AND SERVE: Add the hot pasta right from the colander to the skillet with the sauce. Turn off the heat, stir gently, and allow the pasta to rest for 2 minutes. If the sauce looks thin, gently reduce over low heat for an additional 1 to 2 minutes. If it becomes too thick and jammy, simply thin it out with some of the reserved pasta water. Serve topped with the Parmesan.

prep time: 10 minutes
cook time: about 15 minutes
yield: 4 to 6 servings

CLASSIC CARBONARA

I love the story that this is the pasta that Italian coal miners (aka the *carbonara*) would eat after a long day's work—the ground black pepper is actually supposed to look like a dusting of coal from the mines. My mom does not make this dish often, so I wanted to strike out on my own and come up with a simple version that I could make whenever I wanted. For inspiration and guidance, I turned to a cookbook that my grandmother edited—the 1991 edition of *Joy of Cooking*. (It's so cool that she's kind of with me when I cook, even though she's no longer with us, you know?) The key to the pasta's rich taste is pancetta—which is really just a rolled-up unsmoked cousin of bacon. The sauce is made largely from the hot and starchy pasta water, with cheese (see page 123) and eggs. Keep your focus on integrating them together for the best, creamiest sauce—that's my advice to you. The approach here is fairly traditional, the way Grandma's recipe is—actually, it can be almost complex because it's so simple. Some dishes are like that.

6 ounces **pancetta**, finely diced

Kosher salt

1 pound **spaghetti**

2 large **eggs**, plus 2 large **egg yolks**, lightly beaten

1 cup finely grated **Pecorino cheese**

Freshly ground **black pepper**

2 teaspoons **red wine vinegar**

PANCETTA = ROLLED UP PORK BELLY

CUT SLICES, THEN DICE LIKE THIS

1. COOK THE PANCETTA: Add the pancetta to a large skillet set over medium heat and cook until it's crispy and browned, 3 to 5 minutes, stirring occasionally with a wooden spoon. Use a slotted spoon to remove the pancetta from the fat and set it aside on a paper towel–lined plate to drain. Pour the grease from the skillet into a large serving bowl.

2. COOK THE PASTA: Bring a large pot of water to a rolling boil. Season the water with salt (it should taste like mild seawater), add the spaghetti, and cook, stirring with a slotted spoon to make sure the pasta doesn't clump or stick to the bottom as it cooks, until tender but still chewy, or al dente, 5 to 8 minutes. Set 1 cup of the pasta water aside, then drain the spaghetti in a large colander.

3. SERVE: Add the eggs, egg yolks, and a generous sprinkle of the Pecorino to the bowl with the pancetta grease. Add the hot pasta and use a wooden spoon to mix vigorously so the eggs and cheese coat the pasta. If it's too thick, loosen the pasta with some of the pasta water. Keep in mind, the pasta will be a little loose, and the sauce will thicken as the pasta cools for a few minutes. Think about this: the hot pasta and the water are mixing with the rich eggs, cooking them and making a sauce all at the same time. Simple, but there's a lot going on! Season with pepper and the vinegar. Taste for seasoning. Serve topped with a few turns of pepper, the reserved pancetta, and the remaining Pecorino.

FISH + SHELLFISH

Many home cooks, no matter their age, find cooking fish intimidating because it cooks quickly and can overcook just as fast. It's also fragile, and there are pinbones and skin to navigate. Every fish is slightly different, so mastering its delicate simplicity is something that takes practice. The truth is, though, that the fish and shellfish dishes in this chapter are straightforward and are some of the most delicious recipes to start out with. Plus, they can easily be altered to accommodate whatever type of fish is available where you live. From raw tuna to baked clams to whole roasted bass, this chapter covers a lot of bases.

prep time: 15 minutes
cook time: none
yield: 3 or 4 servings

TUNA CARPACCIO

Carpaccio is a super simple appetizer made from thinly sliced raw fish (or even meats or vegetables) that is laid out on plates and seasoned just before sitting down to eat. Tuna is a classic starting point for carpaccio, although wild salmon is just as good. My mom and I also make a version using ripe and sweet summer tomatoes. Thinly slicing tomatoes as a way of practicing for making carpaccio with fish (pricey farmers' market tomatoes are a lot cheaper than sushi-grade tuna) was helpful for me, so feel free to start there to make it easier to begin. A ripe, juicy tomato of any kind and a large juicy lime are critical. Pick out the produce for this dish carefully (and note that a room-temperature lime will juice easier than a cold one). Sometimes, to make this a complete meal, I'll lay the fish on top of a thin layer of cooked rice, so it's a little like sushi (or nigiri) deconstructed.

½ pound **fresh tuna**, cleaned of any skin or blood (you can ask your fishmonger to do this), very thinly sliced

1 large **beefsteak** or **heirloom tomato**, halved

¼ cup **extra-virgin olive oil**

Juice of 1 large **lime**

Maldon flaky sea salt

1. PLATE THE TUNA: On a large serving platter, arrange the tuna slices in a single layer. Place some of the slices flat and fold some in half so there is a little "life" to the tuna. At this point, you can refrigerate the platter, covered in plastic wrap, for 1 hour and up to 6 hours and finish with the dressing just before serving.

2. MAKE THE DRESSING: Squeeze the tomato halves over a medium bowl so the seeds and juice are expressed from each half. Finely chop the squeezed tomato halves and stir them into the bowl with the seeds and juice. Whisk in the olive oil and lime juice. (This can be done up to 3 to 4 hours before serving—leave at room temperature.)

3. SERVE: When ready to serve, remove the platter from the fridge and spoon the dressing over the fish. Sprinkle generously and evenly with salt.

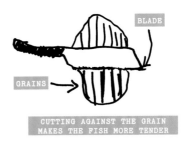

BLADE

GRAINS

CUTTING AGAINST THE GRAIN
MAKES THE FISH MORE TENDER

prep time: 20 minutes
cook time: about 25 minutes
yield: 4 to 6 servings

BAKED CLAMS
with garlic

My dad and I love to share raw clams on the half shell with a squirt of lemon, but my mom only likes clams cooked, so this is a recipe I make for her (even though she takes particular joy in embarrassing me by always bringing up how cute it was when I called clams "clems" when I was a little kid). The heavy cream trick is all hers, though—she taught me that a little cream helps keep the clams juicy under the breadcrumb crust. This is important because breadcrumbs can act like a sponge and just absorb moisture . . . and you don't want dry clams!

40 **littleneck clams**

1 stick (8 tablespoons) **unsalted butter**, softened

2 **scallions**, white and green parts, minced

3 large **garlic cloves**, finely minced

Zest and juice of 1 medium **lemon**

Kosher salt

Freshly ground **black pepper**

⅔ cup **panko breadcrumbs**

¼ cup **plain fine breadcrumbs**

½ to ¾ cup **heavy cream**

½ cup chopped **flat-leaf parsley**

1. Preheat the oven to 375°F.

2. CLEAN THE CLAMS: Clams are still alive when their shells are closed. Soaking any shellfish for long amounts of time in fresh water is not the answer. They live in and only like saltwater. Under cold running water, use a clean and sturdy sponge to scrub and remove sand from the outside of each clam. Rinse a few times in cool water to remove all the sand. There is no shortcut here—the best way to clean clams is with elbow grease and patience!

BREADCRUMB TOPPING

CLAM MEAT

HEAVY CREAM

HALF SHELL

3. COOK THE CLAMS: Heat a large skillet over high heat and add the clams with ½ cup water. Cook, shaking the pan slightly, until the clams open, 3 to 5 minutes. As they open, use a pair of metal tongs to transfer them to a large bowl. Discard any clams that don't open after 5 minutes.

4. MAKE THE TOPPING: In the bowl of a food processor, pulse the butter a few times until it's smooth, then add the scallions, garlic, lemon zest, and half of the lemon juice. Pulse to blend. Transfer the mixture to a medium bowl and season with a pinch of salt and a few turns of pepper. Mix in the breadcrumbs.

5. PREPARE AND BAKE THE CLAMS: Twist the top shell off each clam and discard. Use a small knife and run it under the clam meat to detach it where it is anchored to the bottom shell. If the clams appear sandy on the inside, rinse clean with cool water. Put the meat back in the shell. Pour a touch of the cream on top of each clam and immediately mold about 1 tablespoon of the breadcrumb mixture onto each of the shells so the clam body is totally covered. Arrange them in a single layer on a baking sheet.

6. FINISH: Place the pan in the center of the oven and bake for 12 to 15 minutes until hot and sizzling. Preheat the broiler to high. Leave the clams on the middle rack and broil them for a minute, watching them constantly so they don't burn. Once the topping has browned, remove the pan from the oven. Drizzle the tops with the remaining lemon juice. Sprinkle the clams with the parsley and a pinch of salt and serve immediately.

photographs on pages 138-139

prep time: 15 minutes
cook time: 25 to 30 minutes
yield: 4 servings

LEMON + PECAN-CRUSTED SALMON
with roasted leeks

Salmon has such a wonderfully fatty flavor and tenderness that really takes nicely to the toasty flavors of pecans and breadcrumbs. The combination is like a buttery, toasty salmon sandwich with earthy leeks to boot. My mom turned me on to leeks—I really love their mellow onion flavor. The lemon juice brings out the buttery notes at the end that perks up all the other ingredients.

LEMON-PECAN CRUST

½ stick (4 tablespoons) **unsalted butter**, at room temperature

1 cup **pecan halves**, coarsely chopped

½ cup **panko breadcrumbs**

1 large **lemon**

Kosher salt

LEEKS + SALMON

4 tablespoons **extra-virgin olive oil**

3 large **leeks** (tough outer leaves discarded), halved

Kosher salt

4 (6-ounce) **salmon** fillets, pinbones removed

Freshly ground **black pepper**

1. Preheat the oven to 350°F.

2. MAKE THE LEMON-PECAN CRUST: In a medium bowl, mash the butter with the back of a spoon and mix in the pecans, breadcrumbs, 15 to 18 light grates of lemon zest, and a generous pinch of salt. Cut the lemon in half and reserve for serving.

3. ROAST THE LEEKS: Place a medium oven-safe skillet over medium heat. Add 1 tablespoon of the olive oil and arrange the leek halves, cut side up, in a single layer. Season with a pinch of salt and add another tablespoon of the olive oil and ¼ cup water to the bottom of the pan to create steam as the leeks cook and to prevent them from drying out or burning. Place the pan in the oven to roast until the leeks are tender when pierced with the tip of a knife, 12 to 15 minutes. Remove the pan from the oven.

4. COOK THE FISH: Season the salmon with salt and pepper. Heat a large oven-safe skillet over medium heat and add the remaining 2 tablespoons oil. When the oil begins to smoke lightly, remove the pan from the heat and add the salmon one by one to the pan, skin side down, leaving space between each fillet. Return the pan to the heat and cook until the skin becomes crispy, 3 to 5 minutes. Remove the pan from the heat. If you look at the fish from the side, it will still look raw in the middle.

5. FINISH: Sprinkle and gently press some of the lemon-pecan crust on the top of each piece of fish. Place the pan in the oven and cook until the fish is cooked through, 5 to 8 minutes. The fish is done when it turns a lighter pink-orange color and is no longer translucent in the middle. Remove the pan from the oven and squeeze the lemon halves over the fish. Serve the fish on top of the roasted leeks.

Mom Tips
CLEANING LEEKS

Leeks grow straight up out of the ground like trees, so the dirt can run through the whole vegetable. To clean them, cut the dark green part off the tops and split them down the middle. Wash each half in cold water, letting the dirt rinse out of the layers.

REMOVING PINBONES

Use tweezers to grab the tip of the bone and simply pull it out. Sometimes it's easiest to run your fingers along the length of the fish—you'll feel where the bones are.

prep time: 5 minutes
cook time: 20 to 25 minutes
yield: 4 servings

SWORDFISH
with lemon-caper sauce

You can make this dish using any really steak-y fish you like. Swordfish is my favorite, but it can sometimes be tough to find, and in those instances, we go with striped bass, tuna, cod, or bluefish instead. I have even spooned this sauce over shrimp—and it's excellent! Ava loves capers, and this isn't the only recipe in the book that features them. Capers are briny and salty—if they're too salty for you, soak them for 15 to 20 minutes in cold tap water to tame some of the saltiness. You can also mellow their flavor by lightly frying them in the oil with the fish. Or try using cornichons instead for relish vibes.

LEMON-CAPER SAUCE

½ stick (4 tablespoons) **unsalted butter**, thinly sliced

3 medium **shallots**, cut into ¼-inch-thick rounds

2 dried **bay leaves**

1 tablespoon **brined capers**, drained

Freshly ground **black pepper**

1 cup **dry white wine**

Kosher salt

Zest and juice of 1 **lemon**

SWORDFISH

2 tablespoons **extra-virgin olive oil**

4 (6-ounce) **swordfish** fillets

Kosher salt

1. MAKE THE SAUCE: In a large oven-safe sauté pan, melt 1 tablespoon of the butter over medium-low heat. Add the shallots, bay leaves, capers, and pepper to taste and cook, stirring occasionally with a wooden spoon, until the shallots are translucent and tender, 5 to 8 minutes. Add the wine and reduce until only about 2 tablespoons remain, 3 to 5 minutes. Slowly whisk in the remaining 3 tablespoons butter in small increments. (This is how you make a classic French butter sauce for fish. Adding the butter bit by bit ensures that it won't separate from the other ingredients.) Season with salt and the lemon zest and juice and transfer to a small bowl; discard the bay leaves. Wipe out the pan so you can use it again for the fish.

2. Preheat the oven to 350°F.

3. COOK THE FISH: Heat the pan over medium-high heat and add the olive oil. Season the swordfish with salt. When the oil begins to smoke lightly, remove the pan from the heat and add the swordfish, one by one, to the pan, leaving space between each fillet. Return the pan to the heat and cook until the first side browns, 2 to 3 minutes. Slide a metal spatula under each piece and turn over. Place the pan in the oven and cook until the swordfish is white and no longer translucent in the center, 5 to 8 minutes. (Browning the first side on the stovetop ensures the fish gets enough caramelization for good flavor before being transferred to the oven for gentler roasting until it cooks through.)

4. SERVE: Remove the pan from the oven and spoon the sauce over the swordfish. I like to place the pan right on the table (on an oven mitt or trivet) and serve straight from the pan.

prep time: 10 minutes
cook time: 5 to 7 minutes
yield: 2 to 4 servings

SEARED SCALLOPS
with remoulade

Remoulade is just a fancy French name for a mayonnaise-y sauce that is usually served on salad or fish. The sauce name comes from the word *remolat*, which means "horseradish" in a dialect of French, and, go figure, there isn't even any in this recipe! The capers and parsley are the stars here. They work so well because the mustard and capers in the sauce bring out the natural sweetness of the scallops. It's weird to think of any fish as being sweet, but clams on the half shell, mussels, and scallops all have a great salty note from the ocean and sweetness at the same time. Small capers packed in brine are our house fave, but if you're using large capers, just chop them up before using.

REMOULADE

2 tablespoons **mayonnaise**

1 tablespoon **extra-virgin olive oil**

1 tablespoon **grainy Dijon mustard**

2 teaspoons **brined capers**, drained

1 teaspoon **Sriracha hot sauce**

1 teaspoon **Worcestershire sauce**

6 sprigs of **flat-leaf parsley**, chopped, stems and all

1 large **lemon**, halved

SCALLOPS

2 tablespoons **extra-virgin olive oil**

16 medium-size **diver sea scallops**

Kosher salt

1. MAKE THE REMOULADE: In a medium bowl, stir together the mayonnaise, olive oil, mustard, capers, Sriracha, Worcestershire, parsley, and the juice from half of the lemon. Taste for seasoning.

2. COOK THE SCALLOPS: Heat a large skillet over medium heat and add the olive oil. When the oil begins to smoke lightly, season the scallops with salt, remove the pan from the heat, and add the scallops to the skillet in a single layer. Return the skillet quickly to the heat and cook until the scallops brown on the first side, 2 to 3 minutes. Use a pair of metal tongs to turn the scallops over and cook until browned, 3 to 4 minutes. (If you are more confident, turn the scallops over with a metal spatula; that works fine, too!)

3. SERVE: Place the scallops on a platter or on individual plates. Squeeze the juice from the remaining half of the lemon over them and top each with a little of the sauce.

prep time: 10 minutes
cook time: about 12 minutes
yield: 3 or 4 servings

CLASSIC SHRIMP SCAMPI

This is one of those classic dishes that is perfect on its own—it doesn't need anything more than what it has to offer. A great scampi always allows the subtle sweetness and brininess of the shrimp to coexist peacefully with the garlic and oil. You need some butter to balance the olive oil for the taste of the sauce. Once these ingredients come together, you will understand. Serve with buttered pasta or garlic bread (page 175) or over basmati rice with a little lemon zest stirred in.

2 tablespoons **extra-virgin olive oil**

1½ pounds (about 16 large) **raw shrimp**, shelled and deveined, fresh or thawed if frozen

Kosher salt

3 tablespoons **unsalted butter**

2 large **garlic cloves**, grated

¾ cup **dry white wine**

½ teaspoon **dried red pepper flakes**

2 dashes of **Tabasco**

2 dashes of **Worcestershire sauce**

½ cup **flat-leaf parsley**, stemmed and coarsely chopped

Zest and juice of 1 large **lemon**

¼ cup **panko breadcrumbs**, toasted

1. QUICK-SEAR THE SHRIMP: Heat a large skillet over medium heat and add the olive oil. Season the shrimp on all sides with salt. When the oil begins to smoke lightly, remove the pan from the heat and quickly arrange the shrimp in a single layer, with a little space between each, then return the pan to the heat. Turn up the heat to high and brown the shrimp on their first side, 1 to 2 minutes, adding 1 tablespoon of the butter in small pieces around the shrimp to add flavor as they brown. Turn the shrimp onto their second side and brown for 1 to 2 minutes. The goal here is not to fully cook the shrimp but to brown the exterior and develop flavor. Use a metal spatula or metal tongs to transfer the shrimp to a baking sheet.

2. MAKE THE SAUCE: In the pan where you cooked the shrimp, add the remaining 2 tablespoons butter, garlic, a pinch of salt, and the wine. Simmer over medium heat, stirring, until the wine reduces and the garlic is tender, 3 to 5 minutes. Decrease the heat to low and return the shrimp to the pan, arranging them in the sauce so they can warm through. Use a large spoon to baste the shrimp in the sauce as they warm. Sprinkle with the red pepper flakes. Cook until the shrimp turn pink but are still tender, 2 to 3 minutes. Stir in the Tabasco, Worcestershire, parsley, a few pinches of the lemon zest, and the lemon juice. Taste for seasoning. Sprinkle with the breadcrumbs and serve.

prep time: 10 minutes
cook time: 15 minutes
yield: 2 to 4 servings

WHOLE ROASTED FISH À LA AVA

This dish started with Ava's grandfather. He would practically throw a whole fish like a football right onto a hot baking sheet and just roast it in the oven and serve. It's fun opening the oven and putting the raw fish on the hot pan. It's dramatic—almost like searing something in the oven instead of on top of the stove. Ava loves to check inside the oven and wait for the fish eyes to turn white, a sure sign of doneness. We do this with sea bass, mackerel, bluefish . . . anything that's tasty cooked whole. This is a fish dish that is meant to be messy and enjoyed communally, with people picking pieces of the fish off a platter from the middle of the table, so don't be shy—have at it.

2 whole **black sea bass** (1½ to 2 pounds each), scaled and gutted (ask your fishmonger to do this)

2 large **lemons**, each cut into 7 or 8 rounds

8 sprigs of **thyme** (dill and rosemary are also really good)

¼ cup **extra-virgin olive oil**

Sea salt

Freshly ground **black pepper**

½ cup **flat-leaf parsley** leaves

1. Preheat the oven to 450°F. Line a baking sheet with aluminum foil and place it in the oven to preheat.

2. COOK THE FISH: Stuff the cavities of each fish with the lemon slices and thyme. Rub the olive oil all over the top and bottom of each fish and season on both sides with salt and pepper. Open the oven and place the fish on the hot pan as far as possible from one another (don't remove the pan from the oven—you want it hot). (The distance between the fish, as is true with any protein, will help the fish to brown and roast better.) Cook the fish until tender and the fish flakes at the meatiest part closest to the head, 12 to 15 minutes. The eyes will also turn white—a good visual cue.

3. SERVE: Use a large metal spatula (or two smaller ones) to transfer the fish to a large serving platter. Top with the parsley. Serve immediately.

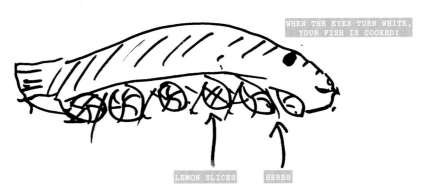

WHEN THE EYES TURN WHITE, YOUR FISH IS COOKED!

LEMON SLICES   HERBS

it's time for some MEAT

Sometimes your kid doesn't feel like your kid. This chapter is about some of those moments for me. Ava loves to eat steak—just like her father. These dishes are ones she could cook and eat every night. If we just tore this chapter out of the book and gave it to Ava, dinner would always be ready. Meat isn't exactly in fashion the way it used to be, and there are plenty of places in this book where vegetables and grains reign supreme. It's nice to enjoy some meat dishes here and there, and these are simple ones to begin your journey, whether you eat meat often or only on occasion.

prep time: 15 minutes
cook time: 55 minutes
yield: 4 to 6 servings

AVA'S COWBOY RIB EYE
+ baked fingerling potatoes

Mom and I have discussed the power of the bay leaf. It adds minty and piney flavor notes to a dish, and here, the bay leaves go so well with the potato skins and the meat itself, it's almost as if they represent, aromatically, what the cow was grazing on (meta, I know). Trust me—this is the right place to use bay leaves, and we put quite a few in with the potatoes. A "cowboy" rib eye means the steak is still on the bone. You can also just use a classic boneless rib eye or strip steak for this recipe. I love to gnaw on the bones the way Mom loves to eat extra cake batter from the bowl.

POTATOES

1½ pounds medium **fingerling potatoes**

2 tablespoons **extra-virgin olive oil**

Maldon flaky sea salt

6 dried or fresh **bay leaves**

1. Preheat the oven to 350°F.

2. BAKE THE POTATOES: Add the potatoes to an oven-safe pot or pan with a fitted lid (make sure the pot is big enough to hold the potatoes) and toss them with the olive oil, a pinch of Maldon salt, and the bay leaves. Cover the pot, place it in the oven, and bake until the potatoes are tender when pierced with the tip of a knife, 25 to 30 minutes. Remove the potatoes from the oven and keep the pot covered until the steak and sauce are finished.

Bay Leaves

If you ever see fresh bay leaves, buy some and store them in the fridge. They are even more tasty and powerful than the dried ones, but either will do in most recipes. If subbing fresh for dried, use half the required amount. The fresh leaves are more potent!

STEAK

4 (8-ounce) bone-in
rib eye steaks

Kosher salt

Freshly ground **black pepper**

2 medium **shallots**,
minced (about ⅓ cup)

1 tablespoon **Dijon mustard**

1 tablespoon
Worcestershire sauce

Zest and juice of
1 small **lemon**

½ cup **beef stock**

2 to 3 tablespoons
heavy cream

8 sprigs of
flat-leaf parsley,
coarsely chopped,
stems and all

3. COOK THE STEAK: Season the steaks on both sides with kosher salt and pepper. Heat a cast-iron skillet that's large enough to hold the four steaks in a single layer over medium-high heat until it begins to visibly smoke. Remove the pan from the heat and use a pair of tongs to place the steaks, one by one, in the dry pan. The fat from the steaks will serve as the oil as they brown. Turn down the heat to medium and return the pan to the heat, then sear the steaks until they are browned on the first side, 6 to 8 minutes. Resist the temptation to turn the steaks over or move them as they cook. Once the first side has a nice crust, turn the steaks over and brown on the second side, 4 to 5 minutes for medium-rare. Remove from the heat and place the steaks on a cutting board to rest while you make the sauce.

4. MAKE THE SAUCE: Remove all but a little bit of grease from the skillet. Add the shallots and cook over medium heat, stirring occasionally, until they are translucent, 3 to 5 minutes. Stir in the mustard, Worcestershire, lemon juice, and zest and swirl the pan so all the flavors start to meld together. Add the stock and reduce until thickened, 3 to 5 minutes. Stir in the cream and parsley and simmer for 1 minute. Taste for seasoning. Place the steaks on four plates with a few potatoes (discard the bay leaves), add a few pinches of Maldon salt, and spoon all the sauce on top.

Note

Sauce making can be different each time. It's important to taste several times as you cook to develop your own eye for how to finish a good sauce. In this recipe, the final cooking liquid is the sauce. If it is too thin, for example, remove the meat and set it aside, then thicken the sauce by simmering it a few extra minutes. Mustard is a natural thickener and flavor enhancer, so that should help. Taste it. Does it need more salt? Pepper? If the sauce is too thick, loosen it with a splash of stock or water.

153   IT'S TIME FOR SOME MEAT

A Note on Doneness

Meat should always be a little less cooked than you would like to allow for carryover cooking. That's the residual heat that rises slightly even after the steak is removed from the pan. This means, if using a meat thermometer, a rare steak will register between 125° and 130°F; medium-rare between 130° and 135°F; and medium between 135° and 140°F. Always insert the thermometer in the thickest part of the steak. You can also make a small incision to check how rare, or pink, the meat is.

prep time: 20 minutes
cook time: 2 to 2½ hours
(mostly inactive time plus
15 minutes for resting)
yield: 4 to 6 servings

BRAISED SHORT RIBS
with red wine + vegetables

If you can master cooking short ribs, you can use the tender meat in all kinds of dishes—from beefy French onion soup, to tacos, pulled-beef sandwiches, and so on. Here, we cook short ribs the classic way with wine and vegetables. Short ribs are a tough cut of meat, so they take time to cook to fork-tender. While you can cook them on the bone or off, here we start super simply: off the bone and with the classic onion-and-carrot accompaniment. You can use larger onions or buy the peeled baby pearl ones (fresh only—not frozen). Good companions to this dish are the Ten-Minute Buttery Egg Noodles (page 117) or the Green Beans Amandine (page 172). We think you will fall in love with the beefiness of this cut.

¼ cup **canola oil**

2 pounds **boneless beef short ribs**, cut into 2-inch cubes

Kosher salt

2 cups **dry red wine**

2 cups peeled **pearl onions**

6 large **garlic cloves**

4 medium **carrots**, cut into 2-inch rounds

4 cups (1 quart) **beef stock**

1 tablespoon **red wine vinegar**

1 tablespoon **Dijon mustard**

1. Preheat the oven to 350°F.

2. BROWN THE BEEF: Heat a Dutch oven over medium heat and add the oil. Arrange the beef cubes in a single layer on a tray and season on all sides with salt. When the oil begins to smoke lightly, remove the pot from the heat and add the beef cubes in a single layer. Return the pot to the heat and cook the meat, undisturbed, until browned, 8 to 10 minutes. Use tongs to turn the meat and continue to brown on all sides for an additional 10 to 12 minutes total. Add the wine and cook until the liquid is reduced to about ¼ cup, 6 to 8 minutes.

3. BRAISE THE BEEF: Add the onions, garlic, carrots, and beef stock along with 2 cups water. Bring the liquid to a simmer over medium heat and use a ladle or a large spoon to skim off any impurities that rise to the surface. Place the pot in the center of the oven and braise until the meat is fork-tender, 1½ to 2 hours (test the meat by flaking it with 2 forks—it should not resist at all when you pull the meat apart; if it does, braise for longer). Remove the pot from the oven and stir in the vinegar and mustard. Taste for seasoning. Allow the meat to rest for 15 minutes before serving.

Mom Tip
DEGLAZING A PAN WITH WINE

If you're adding wine to a pan to deglaze it (ask an adult for help with this step), after adding the wine and using a wooden spoon to scrape all the good bits off the bottom of the pan, let the wine cook out completely before adding more liquid. Otherwise your dish (or sauce) will have a raw wine flavor.

prep time: 15 to 20 minutes
(plus at least 30 minutes for
marinating)
cook time: about 12 minutes
yield: 4 or 5 servings

MARINATED SKIRT STEAK
with feta + herbs

This is almost like a Greek salad but with skirt steak instead of *so many* vegetables (sorry, Mom). You can serve this with marinated cucumbers (page 94) or even just some simple dressed greens (page 36) to catch the drippings and all the wonderful ingredients in the sauce. Skirt steak and hanger steak are thin, cook fast, and have so much taste. Since they're tough cuts that come from the belly, they take to marinating really nicely. In this case, I like to sear and brown the meat a little, marinate it, and then finish cooking it. That way, the meat is browned for flavor, has time to rest in the marinade, and then is cooked the rest of the way and served hot. It's a clever technique. The sharp feta and the earthy rosemary complement the beefy flavor of this particular cut and make the steak taste much fancier than it really is. When you buy feta, buy a small chunk and crumble it yourself at home—feta sold in chunks is often of a better quality and tastier than precrumbled feta.

SKIRT STEAK

4 tablespoons **canola oil**

1½ pounds **skirt steak**,
trimmed of excess fat

Kosher salt

2 tablespoons
Worcestershire sauce

1 tablespoon **Dijon mustard**

1 large **garlic clove**, grated

2 sprigs of **rosemary**, stemmed
and coarsely chopped

1. LIGHTLY SEAR AND MARINATE THE STEAK: Heat a medium cast-iron or heavy-bottomed skillet over medium heat and add 2 tablespoons of the canola oil. Season the steak on both sides with salt. When the oil begins to smoke lightly, remove the pan from the heat and use a pair of tongs to carefully lay the steak in the hot oil in the skillet. Cook it on the first side until browned, about 2 minutes, and then turn it onto the second side and brown it for about 2 minutes more.

2. In a small bowl, stir together the Worcestershire, mustard, garlic, and rosemary. Remove the steak from the skillet (wipe out the pan and set it aside—you will use it again to finish the steak) and place it on a baking sheet lined with parchment paper. It will be barely cooked. Use the back of a spoon to spread the garlic mixture on both sides of the steak and allow it to rest for 10 minutes, then cover with plastic wrap and refrigerate for at least 30 minutes and up to 4 hours.

(recipe and ingredients continue)

RED WINE VINAIGRETTE

2 tablespoons
red wine vinegar

2 tablespoons
extra-virgin olive oil

2 teaspoons **dried oregano**

6 sprigs of **flat-leaf parsley**,
coarsely chopped,
stems and all

4 ounces **creamy feta cheese**
(such as French feta)

3. MAKE THE VINAIGRETTE: In a small bowl, use a whisk to combine the vinegar, olive oil, oregano, and parsley. Crumble in the feta.

4. FINISH THE STEAK: Set the skillet over medium heat and add the remaining 2 tablespoons canola oil. When the oil begins to smoke lightly, remove the pan from the heat and use a pair of metal tongs to add the steaks back to the pan. Cook the meat to your desired doneness: for medium-rare (our favorite way to serve), cook it for 3 to 4 minutes on each side (see page 154). Remove the steak from the skillet and place it on a flat surface. Cut it crosswise and against the grain to ensure you have tender slices. Serve topped with the feta vinaigrette.

Note

Cast iron gives such a great, even heat and a good sear to meat. While browning meat, such as in step 1 of this recipe, does *not* lock in any juices, it does make your dishes taste better, because the point of browning is to add flavor!

prep time: 20 minutes
cook time: 60 to
70 minutes
(mostly inactive)
yield: 4 servings

WHOLE ROASTED CHICKEN
with potatoes

My mom says this chicken tastes like being in Paris (eye roll). But I have to admit—it is pretty perfect. And all you need are a few select ingredients and the right equipment. Here, I use a roasting pan with low sides and also a roasting rack to elevate the bird for maximum browning of the skin. For flavor, you can certainly go classic and use carrots, onions, and celery, but I always want some potatoes (they taste so good with the roasted chicken skin). Grainy mustard offers a vinegary note that I learned to appreciate from my mom, who learned it from years of cooking bistro food in France. I sometimes resist her choices, but I have to admit, I love the pop of the vinegary mustard seeds here. The seeds are almost bitter in a pleasant way.

2 large **Idaho** or **russet potatoes**, scrubbed clean and cut into 1-inch-thick rounds

2 to 3 tablespoons **extra-virgin olive oil**

Kosher salt

1 (3½- to 4-pound) **whole chicken**

Freshly ground **black pepper**

1 cup **chicken stock**

1 tablespoon **grainy Dijon mustard**

1. Preheat the oven to 400°F.

2. ROAST THE CHICKEN: Arrange the potato slices in the bottom of a roasting pan with low sides. Drizzle the potatoes with the olive oil and a pinch of salt. Place the chicken, breast side up, on a roasting rack, season with salt and pepper, and place the rack in the center of the pan and on top of the potatoes. Place the pan on the center rack of the oven and roast until the juices run clear in the leg/thigh joint or a meat thermometer inserted into the thickest part of the thigh registers 165°F, 55 to 65 minutes. Remove the roasting pan from the oven. Remove the chicken from the pan and gently place it, breast side down, on a cutting board so the juices can flow through the breast meat as it rests for 10 to 15 minutes. Remove the potatoes from the pan and set aside.

3. MAKE THE SAUCE: Place the roasting pan on a burner on the stove and add the chicken stock and mustard. Simmer gently over medium heat, using a wooden spoon or heat-resistant rubber spatula to scrape up the bits and skin from the bottom of the pan. Let the sauce simmer until it becomes slightly thick and tasty, 3 to 5 minutes. Taste for seasoning.

4. SERVE: Turn the chicken over so it's breast side up and carve (an adult comes in handy here your first few times). As you cut the breast meat off, place it on a serving platter and spoon a little sauce directly onto the flesh part, a special touch that boosts the flavor. Taste the meat and season only if needed. Serve with the potatoes on the side.

photographs on pages 162–163

prep time: 10 minutes
cook time: 12 to 15 minutes
yield: 4 servings

BEEF TENDERLOIN
AU POIVRE

The word *poivre* means "pepper" in French, and when you make a pepper-crusted steak, it's almost as much about the texture of the pepper with the meat as it is about its spiciness. For a true au poivre vibe, put the whole peppercorns on a cutting board and use the bottom of a heavy-duty small sauté pan to crush the peppercorns. It's okay if some are crushed more finely than others—it's part of what gives the pepper such power in this dish. You want a variety of coarse and fine bits to bite into. These steaks cook surprisingly fast because each is only about 6 ounces *and* tenderloin is a lean cut—meaning there isn't a lot of fat insulating it (also meaning—take care not to overcook it!). Try serving it with Green Beans Amandine (page 172).

4 (6- to 7-ounce) 1½-inch-thick **beef tenderloin steaks**

Kosher salt

2 tablespoons **black peppercorns**, coarsely cracked

2 tablespoons **canola oil**

2 large **garlic cloves**, grated

1 tablespoon **Dijon mustard**

1 tablespoon **Worcestershire sauce**

1 cup **beef stock**

Maldon flaky sea salt

1. GET READY: Season the steaks generously on both sides with kosher salt. Add the pepper to a plate and roll each steak in the pepper, generously coating all sides. Press the pepper into the meat to make sure it sticks.

2. COOK THE STEAK: Heat a cast-iron or heavy-bottomed skillet over medium heat and add the oil. When the oil begins to smoke lightly, remove the pan from the heat and use a pair of tongs to carefully set the steaks in the hot oil, making sure to leave space between each piece. Return the pan to the heat and cook them on the first side for 2 to 3 minutes until browned and then turn them onto the second side and cook for another 2 to 3 minutes (your kitchen will get smoky—that's okay!). Use a meat thermometer to check for doneness (see page 154). If you like your steak more on the well-done side, leave it in the pan for 2 to 3 minutes longer on each side.

3. MAKE THE SAUCE: In a small bowl, stir together the garlic, mustard, and Worcestershire. Decrease the heat to medium-low and add the garlic mixture to the pan, swirling around the meat and spooning the sauce over it too. Use tongs to transfer the steaks to a plate (leave the sauce in the pan) and set aside to rest for a few minutes. Add the stock to the pan and simmer over medium heat until the sauce thickens slightly, 3 to 5 minutes. Taste for seasoning.

4. SERVE: Serve the steaks with the sauce on individual plates or family style on a platter. Finish with a sprinkle of Maldon salt.

PEPPERCORNS

CUTTING BOARD

prep time: 15 minutes
cook time: 20 to 25 minutes
yield: 2 servings

CAST-IRON PAPRIKA CHICKEN

You can tell which chicken recipe came from whom by the cut: chicken breast recipes are Mom's, and any chicken thigh and drumstick recipes are mine! You can use a sweet, smoky paprika or a spicy one here, depending on your flavor preference. Besides heat and smoke, paprika also lends a deep red-brown color to the chicken—it's super appealing. The trick to great chicken dinners is learning when the chicken is cooked through and safe to eat but not overcooked and dried out. In this case, that happens when the chicken registers 165°F on a meat thermometer inserted into the thickest part of the breast.

2 (5- to 6-ounce) **boneless, skin-on chicken breasts**

Kosher salt

½ teaspoon **sweet, smoky, or hot paprika**

2 tablespoons **extra-virgin olive oil**

2 large **garlic cloves**, grated

1 small **yellow onion**, halved and thinly sliced

½ pound (8 ounces) **white button mushrooms**, stemmed and sliced

½ cup **dry white wine**

Zest and juice of 1 large **lemon**

1. SEASON THE CHICKEN: Season both sides of the chicken breasts with a sprinkle of salt and use a small fine-mesh strainer to dust the chicken with the paprika. (You can always get an even coating of powdered spices on anything if you "crop dust" by putting the spice in a small strainer and sprinkling.)

2. COOK THE CHICKEN: Heat 2 tablespoons of the olive oil in a large cast-iron skillet over medium heat until it smokes lightly. Remove the pan from the heat and add the chicken breasts, rounded side down, leaving a little space between them. Return the pan to the heat and cook until golden brown, 5 to 7 minutes. Use a pair of metal tongs or a metal spatula to flip the chicken to its second side and cook until a meat thermometer inserted into the thickest part registers 165°F, 5 to 7 additional minutes. Transfer the chicken to a plate to rest while you make the sauce. Don't wash the pan—you will use it to make the sauce.

3. MAKE THE SAUCE: Discard all but a little bit of grease from the pan. Add the garlic, onion, mushrooms, and a pinch of salt. Cook over medium heat until the mushrooms are tender, 3 to 5 minutes. Add the wine and reduce until almost all the liquid cooks down. Stir in a splash of water and the lemon zest and juice. Taste for seasoning and reduce the heat to medium-low.

4. SERVE: Place the breasts in the sauce and spoon the sauce over the meat, warming it gently so it stays moist. Serve with the sauce.

prep time: 5 minutes
cook time: about 25 minutes
yield: 2 servings

MUSTARDY CHICKEN THIGHS

As I said earlier, chicken breasts are my mom's jam, and chicken thighs are so me. A chicken thigh is an almost perfect food to me. It's got a super crispy skin when cooked right (meaning a great texture), and the dark meat from the thigh has more flavor than the breast meat. I like to slather the thighs with Dijon mustard and cook them over pretty high heat. There are some recipes that don't have a lot of ingredients but whose flavor really goes a long way—this is one of those recipes. Chicken thighs need to be cooked until their juices run clear. If there's any trace of pink in the juices, you know they aren't cooked enough.

4 large (about 1¼ pounds total) **bone-in, skin-on chicken thighs**

Kosher salt

2 tablespoons **Dijon mustard**

2 tablespoons **canola oil**

Rice, **green beans** (page 172), or **marinated cucumbers** (page 94), for serving

1. Preheat the oven to 350°F.

2. SEASON THE CHICKEN: Arrange the chicken on a baking sheet in a single layer and season with salt. Turn over the pieces and season again. Spread the mustard generously over the flesh side of the chicken thighs.

3. COOK THE CHICKEN: Heat a large heavy-bottomed oven-safe skillet over high heat. Add the oil. When the oil begins to smoke lightly, remove the skillet from the heat and add the chicken, skin side down. Do not overcrowd the pan. Return the pan to the heat and allow the thighs to brown for 5 to 8 minutes, resisting the temptation to move or turn the pieces. Use tongs to turn over the chicken and brown on the second side, 3 to 5 minutes. Place the pan in the oven and cook for 8 to 10 minutes more or until a meat thermometer inserted into the center of a thigh registers 165°F.

4. SERVE: Serve the chicken on a bed of rice, with green beans or marinated cucumbers.

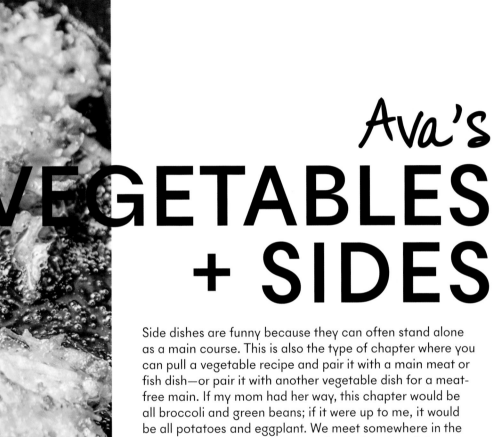

Ava's
VEGETABLES
+ SIDES

Side dishes are funny because they can often stand alone as a main course. This is also the type of chapter where you can pull a vegetable recipe and pair it with a main meat or fish dish—or pair it with another vegetable dish for a meat-free main. If my mom had her way, this chapter would be all broccoli and green beans; if it were up to me, it would be all potatoes and eggplant. We meet somewhere in the middle here with a bunch of our family favorites. We get inspo from our shopping, like at a farm stand, greenmarket, or supermarket; from the time of year; and from what we just feel like eating. Our hope is that you take away some clever tricks for cooking and serving vegetables and get closer to understanding which ones you specifically love to cook and eat.

prep time: 10 minutes
cook time: 8 to 10 minutes
yield: 4 or 5 servings

GREEN BEANS AMANDINE

This is a French bistro classic. *Amandine* just means that it's made with almonds and (usually) some butter. My mom loves it when I eat green vegetables, and I love it when they can be mixed with some of my favorite things, such as butter, capers, and olive oil–toasted almonds. These green beans go great with shrimp or other fish dishes, any of the beef dishes from the meat chapter (especially the beef tenderloin on page 165), or even some of the egg dishes in the breakfast chapter like the sausage frittata on page 29.

4 tablespoons **extra-virgin olive oil**

1 tablespoon **red wine vinegar**

1 tablespoon **grainy Dijon mustard**

1 tablespoon **cool water**

1 teaspoon **brined capers**, plus a little brine

Kosher salt

Freshly ground **black pepper**

1 pound **green beans** (preferably thin ones), ends trimmed

½ cup **sliced almonds**

2 tablespoons **unsalted butter**

1. MAKE THE DRESSING: In a medium bowl, whisk together 2 tablespoons of the olive oil, the vinegar, mustard, and water until smooth. Add the capers, a splash of brine, a pinch of salt, and 2 turns of pepper. Taste for seasoning.

2. BLANCH THE GREEN BEANS: Bring a medium pot of water to a boil. Season the water with salt (it should taste like mild seawater). Prepare an ice bath by filling a bowl large enough to hold the green beans with cold water. Add some ice cubes and set aside. Stir the green beans into the boiling water and allow them to cook until crisp-tender, 2 to 3 minutes. Use a slotted spoon to remove them from the water, transferring them immediately to the ice bath. Allow them to sit in the ice bath for a few minutes, swirling them gently in the water until they are fully cooled. Drain and transfer the green beans to a kitchen towel set on a flat surface and thoroughly pat them dry.

3. BROWN THE ALMONDS: Line a baking sheet with paper towels. Heat a large skillet over medium heat and add the remaining 2 tablespoons olive oil. When the oil is hot, sprinkle the almonds into the pan in a single layer and fry them, stirring constantly, until they turn light brown. This will happen fast. Season them generously with salt and use a slotted spoon to transfer them to the prepared baking sheet.

4. COOK THE GREEN BEANS: Heat the same skillet over medium heat and add the butter. When the butter melts and gets foamy, add the green beans. Season them with salt and cook, stirring, 2 to 3 minutes. Stir in the dressing and almonds. Taste for seasoning.

prep time: 10 minutes
cook time: about 40 minutes
yield: 4 to 6 servings

SHALLOT-GARLIC BREAD

Garlic bread in our house is a *thing.* Garlic, herbs, and butter are all ingredients that become their best selves when in the company of sweet shallots, and this recipe rolls them all together in one. Sometimes, when we are extra organized, we roll this up the night before, let it marinate in the fridge, and just pop it into the oven the next day. Ava jokes that we don't need scented candles anymore, just this shallot-garlic bread!

2 tablespoons **extra-virgin olive oil**

2 medium **shallots**, cut into thin rounds

5 large **garlic cloves**, grated

Kosher salt

1 (13-inch) loaf **Italian bread**

½ stick (4 tablespoons) **unsalted butter**, thinly sliced

1 tablespoon **garlic powder**

1 tablespoon **Maldon flaky sea salt**

Freshly ground **black pepper**

10 sprigs of **flat-leaf parsley**, coarsely chopped, stems and all

1. GET READY: In a medium skillet, warm the olive oil over medium heat. Add the shallots, garlic, and a pinch of kosher salt. Cook, stirring occasionally, until tender, 3 to 5 minutes. Turn off the heat.

2. Preheat the oven to 350°F.

3. PREPARE THE BREAD: Cut the bread crosswise into ¾-inch slices, top each slice with butter and then divide the shallot-garlic mixture (including the infused oil) over the butter. Sprinkle with garlic powder, flaky salt, some pepper, and the parsley. Reassemble the slices into a loaf and wrap it tightly with aluminum foil. (You can also slice the bread in half lengthwise, as if you are making an oversized sandwich, top each half with the butter, shallot-garlic mixture, and spices, then close the bread before wrapping it in foil. See the illustration below.)

4. BAKE: Place the foil-wrapped loaf on a baking sheet and bake until hot to the touch, 25 to 30 minutes. Remove the bread from the oven, open the foil (be careful of the steam!), and arrange the slices, topping side up, on the foil. Return the bread to the oven and bake for 5 to 8 minutes so the exterior becomes crispy. Remove from the oven and serve immediately.

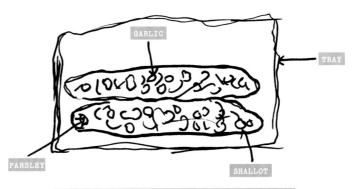

SPREAD TOPPINGS SO EVERY BITE HAS EVERY FLAVOR!

prep time: 20 minutes
cook time: about 40 minutes
yield: 9 or 10 latkes

NANNY IDA'S POTATO LATKES

I love that my mom's side of the family is Italian American, and my father's is Jewish. My dad always calls me a pizza bagel for that reason. I used to make latkes with my grandmother (my nanny), but in the past couple of years, I got the hang of them enough to make them myself, while she and Pop watched. I never met my great-grandmother Ida, but she's the one who taught my nanny how to make latkes. My grandmother says that Nanny Ida was a very "layered" and "spicy" person, in a good way. I like that idea. It's also cool to think of a special person when you cook a dish. These latkes, with their crunchy, potato-y layers (thanks to pan searing and then finishing in the oven) and hints of garlic and onion powder, taste like that feeling to me.

1 medium **white onion**

4 large **russet potatoes**, peeled

2 large **eggs**

2 tablespoons **cornstarch**

1 tablespoon **garlic powder**

1 tablespoon **onion powder**

Kosher salt

Freshly ground **black pepper**

6 tablespoons **canola oil**

1. PREPARE THE POTATOES: Grate the onion and then the potatoes on the largest-hole side of a box grater. Put the shredded potatoes and onion in a bowl of cold water to wash off the starch. Rinse a few times, draining the water and washing off the starch. Drain and place on a sturdy kitchen towel. Twist up the towel and wring out all the water.

2. Preheat the oven to 350°F. Line a baking sheet with parchment paper.

3. MAKE THE POTATO MIX: In a large bowl, whisk together the eggs and cornstarch until smooth. Mix in the potato and onion mixture, garlic powder, and onion powder, and season generously with salt and pepper.

4. FORM THE LATKES: Add 3 tablespoons of the oil to a large cast-iron skillet set over medium heat and swirl it around to coat the bottom and sides. When the oil begins to smoke lightly, remove the pan from the heat. Use a ¼-cup measure to add small cakes of the potato mixture to the pan, using up half of the mixture and leaving about 1 inch of space between each cake. Return the pan to the heat and cook until browned on the first side. Use a metal spatula to press down gently on the potato cakes so they're about ½ to ¾ inch thick and to make sure the potatoes stick together.

(recipe continues)

5. BAKE THE LATKES: Increase the heat to medium-high and cook until the water starts to release from the potatoes and you can see the edges browning, 6 to 8 minutes. Flip the latkes and immediately place the skillet in the oven and bake, undisturbed, for 8 to 10 minutes or until the latkes feel hard and crispy and are golden brown. If they're not, return to the oven for a few additional minutes of cooking. Remove the latkes from the oven, season immediately with salt, and transfer to the prepared baking sheet. While the first batch is baking, make the remaining batch. Before you start, pour off any liquid in the pan and wipe out any potato bits that might burn. Return the pan to the burner, heat the remaining 3 tablespoons oil, and cook the remaining potato mixture the same way.

LATKES

LEAVE SPACE BETWEEN EACH LATKE
SO THEY BROWN WELL

prep time: 5 minutes
cook time: 45 minutes
(plus 15 minutes for resting)
yield: 6 to 8 servings

SLOW-COOKED FARRO
with balsamic

Farro looks like rice but is actually dried wheat. You can make a risotto-type dish with it, or you can approach it more simply, as in this recipe, which my mom taught me. Farro takes a little while to cook (longer than you may think), but its nuttiness and texture make it worth the wait since it's so satisfying to eat. I like to cook farro in water so you get its full and pure flavor, but you can also cook it in stock or bone broth for a meatier taste. It's an excellent companion to the whole fish on page 148 or the paprika chicken cutlets on page 166, or can even be used as a base for a grain bowl that's topped with roasted vegetables.

2 tablespoons **extra-virgin olive oil**

2 medium **shallots**, cut into thin rounds

Kosher salt

1 cup **farro**

1 tablespoon **balsamic vinegar**

1. Preheat the oven to 350°F.

2. COOK THE FARRO: Heat a large sauté pan over medium heat and add the olive oil and shallots with about 1 tablespoon salt. Cook, stirring occasionally, until the shallots become translucent, 3 to 5 minutes. Stir in the farro and cook for 2 minutes, until you hear it crackle. Add 3½ cups water. Stir gently and bring to a simmer. Cover and place in the oven. Cook, stirring from time to time, for 35 to 40 minutes or until the grains fluff slightly and separate and the farro has a little bite like al dente pasta but is tender when you start to chew. If it has too much chew, add a splash more water and cook it a while longer until it becomes more tender.

3. FINISH: Remove the pan from the oven. Stir in the vinegar and let the farro sit for 10 to 15 minutes. Use a large spoon to stir it a few times to mix the flavors, then taste for seasoning.

prep time: 10 minutes
(plus 1 hour marinating)
cook time: 2 to 3 minutes
yield: 4 to 6 servings

MY GRANDPA'S BROCCOLI
with balsamic

My grandpa used the same vinaigrette to dress hearty and bitter salad greens as he used for his tour de force—this broccoli. He'd hobble to the fridge and pull out the marinated broccoli (he always chilled it for at least 1 hour before serving), beaming with pride as my mom, grandma, and I devoured the whole plate. My mom's parents are no longer with us, and as silly as it may sound, this simple broccoli is one of my strongest food memories. It's one of the only dishes my grandfather actually cooked for me. The rest of the cooking is just what my mom shares from her own memories. Grandpa showed me how you can cut the broccoli into spears so the stems remain intact and how to peel the stems so they look like makeshift asparagus spears. Peeling the stems makes them so much more tender and appealing to eat. This also makes your broccoli dish look and taste more unusual. You could make this dish with cauliflower or asparagus, too. For fun add-ons, top with some crispy onions or shallots or even some chopped pecans.

2 pounds **broccoli** (about 2 heads), ends trimmed

3 tablespoons **balsamic vinegar**

1 medium **garlic clove**, grated

1 teaspoon **garlic powder**

Kosher salt

2 tablespoons **extra-virgin olive oil**

1. PREPARE THE BROCCOLI: Cut the broccoli into long pieces, keeping a little of the floret and a piece of the stem on each so they look a little like asparagus (see page 182). Use a vegetable peeler to peel any outer skin off the stem parts and smooth any edges.

2. MAKE THE VINAIGRETTE: In a medium bowl, whisk together the vinegar, garlic, garlic powder, and a pinch of salt. Slowly whisk in the olive oil until the mixture is thick and emulsified. Taste for seasoning.

3. COOK THE BROCCOLI: Bring a large pot of water to a boil. Season the water with salt (it should taste like mild seawater). Prepare an ice bath by filling a bowl large enough to hold the broccoli with cold water. Add some ice cubes and set aside. Stir the broccoli into the boiling water and allow it to cook until crisp-tender, 2 to 3 minutes. Use a slotted spoon to transfer the broccoli to the ice bath. Allow it to sit for a few minutes, swirling it gently in the water until it is fully cooled. Transfer the broccoli to a kitchen towel, set on a flat surface, and thoroughly pat dry.

4. FINISH: Arrange the broccoli on a platter in a single layer and spoon the dressing all over it. Refrigerate for at least 1 hour and up to 6 hours to let the broccoli absorb the flavors of the vinaigrette. Spoon the dressing that has pooled on the platter back over the broccoli right before serving.

photographs on pages 182-183

prep time: 15 minutes
cook time: 40 to 50 minutes
yield: 4 to 6 servings

BRAISED SAVOY CABBAGE
with tomato + spices

This is one of the few distinctly Indian dishes my mom makes from time to time from one of Julie Sahni's Indian cookbooks. When braised with cumin, caraway, and coriander, savoy cabbage becomes meltingly tender, tangy from the tomato, and super flavorful because of the spices. While the cumin and caraway are whole, the coriander is lightly crushed since the seeds are larger. Crushing whole spices can also enhance the flavor they give. Crushed coriander is super floral. Simply put the seeds on a cutting board and use the bottom of a heavy-bottomed sauté pan to lightly crush open the seeds. This dish would be a great companion to the whole roasted chicken (page 161), but I also love it served with a baked potato and sour cream for a hearty vegetarian dinner. Don't like cilantro? Leave it out. My mom says she didn't like cilantro until she was thirty!

2 teaspoons **coriander seeds**

2 tablespoons **unsalted butter**

2 teaspoons **cumin seeds**

2 teaspoons **caraway seeds**

1 small head of **savoy cabbage**, cored and thinly sliced

Kosher salt

Freshly ground **black pepper**

1 (14.5-ounce) can **whole peeled tomatoes**

1 tablespoon finely grated **ginger**

6 sprigs of **cilantro**, finely chopped, stems and all

1 tablespoon **red wine vinegar**

1. TOAST THE SPICES: Place the coriander seeds on a cutting board and lightly crush them with the bottom of a sauté pan or Dutch oven. In a large sauté pan, melt the butter over medium heat. Add the cumin, caraway, and crushed coriander and toast them slightly in the butter, stirring occasionally, for 30 seconds.

2. COOK THE CABBAGE: Immediately add the cabbage. Toss to coat with the butter and spices and season with a pinch of salt and some pepper. Cook, stirring from time to time, until the cabbage starts to break down, 8 to 10 minutes. Lightly crush the tomatoes with your fingers. Add the ginger and the tomatoes with their liquid and cook for an additional 8 to 10 minutes, stirring occasionally, until the tomatoes meld with the cabbage. Taste for seasoning.

3. FINISH THE DISH: Reduce the heat to low and add the cilantro and vinegar. Bring to a simmer over medium-low heat and cook until the cabbage is tender, 25 to 30 minutes. Serve warm.

Toasting Spices

You can toast spices to wake up the oils and flavors in a few different ways. My two favorite approaches: Spread the spices out on a baking sheet and toast in a 350°F oven for 2 to 3 minutes, or bloom the spices in hot butter or oil, as in this recipe.

prep time: 10 minutes
cook time: 25 to 30 minutes
yield: 4 to 6 servings

TRIPLE-COOKED POTATOES

This recipe has Ava written all over it. Her favorite vegetable is definitely potatoes. If left to her own devices, every night's dinner would be a cowboy rib eye (page 152) with these crispy, super-potato-y potatoes. They're so simple. The trick is to plump the potatoes by almost fully cooking them in water before panfrying them in a cast-iron skillet and finishing in the oven (with the pan on the rack in the lowest position or even on the *floor* of the oven!) with a little oil so they develop a golden, crunchy crust.

1½ to 2 pounds medium **red bliss potatoes**

Kosher salt

Extra-virgin olive oil

4 sprigs of **thyme**

Maldon flaky sea salt

1. COOK THE POTATOES: Place the potatoes in a large pot and cover with cold water. Bring the water to a boil over high heat, then reduce to a simmer. Add a generous pinch of kosher salt and allow the potatoes to cook until tender when pierced with the tip of a knife, 20 to 25 minutes. Drain in a colander, place them on a flat surface, and use the side of a wooden spoon to press/smash them gently to flatten.

2. Preheat the oven to 400°F. Set one oven rack in the lowest position.

3. BROWN AND SERVE: Add enough olive oil to a large oven-safe skillet (preferably cast-iron) to fill it by ½ inch. Heat the oil over medium heat until it begins to smoke lightly. Remove the pan from the heat and arrange the potatoes in a single layer. Add the thyme sprigs to the pan. Use the side of a wooden spoon or sturdy metal spatula to press on the potatoes to flatten them even more. Return the pan to the heat and brown the potatoes slowly, 3 to 5 minutes. Use a pair of tongs to turn each potato over, and place the pan in the oven. Roast until the potatoes are well browned, 8 to 10 minutes. Season generously with flaky salt. Serve immediately.

Mom Tip

If some potatoes are larger, drop them in the water first, cook for 5 minutes, and then add the smaller ones so they all finish cooking at the same time.

LEAVE A LITTLE SPACE BETWEEN EACH POTATO

ARRANGE POTATOES IN A SINGLE LAYER FOR BETTER BROWNING

DESSERTS

While Ava is not much of a dessert person, she does like something sweet when she's in the mood for it, and what's a cookbook without a few indulgences to end a meal with? Some of these recipes, like the Pumpkin Bread (page 194) or the Black + White Cupcakes (page 220), are great for a brunch. Others, like the banana icebox cake (page 199) or the strawberry crisp (page 202), feel more late-afternoon dessert-y. Then, there are also a few showstoppers, like the pavlova (page 190) and the blueberry pie (page 214). What do they all have in common? They all use techniques that you can learn and then apply to other recipes. For example, use the chocolate mousse on page 205 as a filling for the birthday cake on page 222. These are building block recipes that can serve so many different moments. After all, dessert is about more than just being hungry—as Ava might say, "Mom, dessert is a *mood.*"

prep time: 20 minutes
(plus at least 2 hours for macerating)
cook time: 1 hour
yield: 8 servings

PAVLOVA
with strawberries

This is a Grandma recipe that got passed down to Mom, and now I run with it. While my mom likes to say that my idea of a perfect dessert is a giant steak and a baked potato, I do have a soft spot for classic French desserts like this one. French sweets often mix together rich components and then balance them out with some acidic fruit. This pavlova is one of my absolute favorites because it combines so many textures and flavors—from the pillowy baked meringue to the seeds from the strawberries, from the tartness of the raspberry jam to the sweet richness of vanilla whipped cream, all are divine together. You can make the meringues early in the day and serve them that night, but otherwise, this is not a dessert that keeps well. Make and enjoy the pavlovas right away!

3 pints of **strawberries**, hulled and halved

1 tablespoon **raspberry jam**

1 tablespoon **lemon zest** and 2 tablespoons **lemon juice** (from 1 lemon)

¼ cup packed **dark brown sugar**

Nonstick cooking spray

1 cup **granulated sugar**

2 teaspoons **cornstarch**

4 large **egg whites**, at room temperature

½ teaspoon **cream of tartar**

1½ cups **heavy cream**

1 **vanilla bean**, split lengthwise and scraped of inner seeds, or 1 teaspoon **vanilla extract**

1. MACERATE THE FRUIT: Add the strawberries and raspberry jam to a medium bowl along with the lemon zest and juice. Add the brown sugar and gently toss to combine. Cover with plastic wrap and refrigerate for at least 2 hours and up to 6 hours.

2. GET THE OVEN READY FOR THE MERINGUE: Position two racks in the upper third of the oven and preheat it to 200°F. Line two baking sheets with parchment paper and lightly coat with cooking spray.

3. MAKE THE MERINGUE: In a medium bowl, whisk together the granulated sugar and cornstarch. In the bowl of an electric mixer fitted with the whisk attachment, beat the egg whites and the cream of tartar at high speed until the egg whites hold their shape and the whisk leaves a trace in the whites, about 2 minutes. Reduce the mixer speed to medium and start adding the sugar mixture, tablespoon by tablespoon, waiting until each spoonful is incorporated before adding more. After 3 to 5 additional minutes, the meringue should be firm and glossy and hold stiff peaks. Scrape down the sides of the bowl with a spatula to ensure the meringue is even in consistency.

4. BAKE THE MERINGUE: Spoon the meringue into eight even, individual rounds (about 2 inches in diameter) on the prepared baking sheets, four on each. You can neaten the edges of the circles and even wipe away or clean up the edges of the circles with a clean kitchen towel. Place the sheets in the oven and bake, undisturbed, for 30 minutes. After 30 minutes, rotate the baking sheets front to back, swap racks, and bake for an additional 30 minutes. Turn off the oven and allow the meringues to cool completely in the oven for 15 to 20 minutes. (Once cooled, the meringues will keep for a few hours, but they're best served soon after cooling.)

5. MAKE THE CREAM AND PREPARE THE FRUIT: In the cleaned bowl of the mixer, using the cleaned whisk attachment, beat the cream and vanilla seeds on medium-high speed until you have somewhat stiff peaks. Spoon the fruit onto the bottom of a serving platter and gently place the meringues on top. Serve with a bowl of the whipped cream on the side.

photographs on pages 192–193

prep time: 15 minutes (plus cooling)
cook time: 1 hour 30 minutes
yield: 1 (8½ x 4½-inch) loaf

PUMPKIN BREAD

Halloween and Thanksgiving are probably our favorite holidays for making desserts because we both love pumpkin and squash. I have roasted my fair share of fresh squash, but there's no need to go through the peeling, seeding, and roasting when canned pumpkin offers great results in a fraction of the time. I also find this to be a great way to share the spices and tastes from the holiday season at any time of the year. Ava and I look forward to this pumpkin bread's welcoming array of warm spicy flavors and its surprisingly light texture. Ava's little chef-y contribution here? We use olive oil instead of a neutral oil or butter. We love the grassy note of the oil paired with the earthy flavor of the pumpkin. The pumpkin puree, much like applesauce, adds such moisture to the bread that it gives it excellent staying power—it's as good on day four as it is on day one, if it even hangs around that long.

PUMPKIN BREAD

1 tablespoon **unsalted butter**, softened

1 (15-ounce) can **pumpkin puree** (not pie filling)

½ cup **extra-virgin olive oil**

3 large **eggs**, lightly beaten

1⅔ cups **granulated sugar**

⅓ cup packed **dark brown sugar**

1½ teaspoons **baking powder**

¾ teaspoon **baking soda**

1 teaspoon **kosher salt**

1 teaspoon ground **cinnamon**

½ teaspoon ground **ginger**

¼ teaspoon **nutmeg** (preferably freshly grated)

¼ teaspoon ground **cloves**

2¼ cups **all-purpose flour**

1 teaspoon **apple cider vinegar**

TOPPING

1 tablespoon **granulated sugar**

1 teaspoon ground **cinnamon**

1. GET READY: Preheat the oven to 350°F. Use the softened butter to grease the bottom and sides of an 8½ x 4½-inch (6 cup) loaf pan.

2. MAKE THE PUMPKIN BREAD BATTER: In a large bowl, whisk together the pumpkin, olive oil, eggs, and sugars until smooth. Sprinkle the baking powder, baking soda, salt, cinnamon, ginger, nutmeg, and cloves over the batter and whisk until well combined. Add the flour and stir with a wooden spoon just until mixed. Whisk in the vinegar just until incorporated. Scrape into the prepared pan and smooth the top.

3. MAKE THE TOPPING: In a small dish or measuring cup, stir the granulated sugar and cinnamon together. Sprinkle over the top of the batter.

4. BAKE: Place the loaf pan in the center of the oven and bake for 65 to 75 minutes until a tester poked into all parts of the bread (both the top and center will want to hide pockets of uncooked batter) comes out batter-free.

5. COOL: Cool the bread in the pan for 30 minutes and then remove from the pan and set on a cutting board. Cool completely and slice crosswise like a loaf of bread. Cover in plastic wrap and store on the counter overnight. After that, refrigerate for up to a few days.

prep time: 15 to 20 minutes (plus cooling)
cook time: 20 minutes
yield: 18 cookies

DARK CHOCOLATE COOKIES

This is one of the first recipes I ever made in a professional kitchen. These were the bookend cookies for a peanut butter ice cream sandwich that was to die for. The combination of chocolates in the cookie is key because the unsweetened chocolate offers a pleasant bitterness while the semisweet offers that almost candy-bar brownie sweetness I always crave. They have a deep cocoa-y note and a slightly chewy, moist center. For the chocolate, it's better to chop the chocolate from a bar (Lindt or Ghirardelli, for example) than to use chips.

3 tablespoons **unsalted butter**, cut into pieces, plus extra for greasing

2.5 ounces **semisweet chocolate** (½ cup plus 1 tablespoon), coarsely chopped

1.5 ounces **unsweetened chocolate** (⅓ cup), coarsely chopped

1 large **egg**

1 cup **sugar**

1 teaspoon **vanilla extract**

¼ cup **all-purpose flour**

½ teaspoon **baking powder**

⅓ cup **Dutch-processed cocoa powder**

1 teaspoon **kosher salt**

1. Preheat the oven to 350°F. Grease two baking sheets with butter (don't bake the cookies on parchment).

2. MELT THE CHOCOLATE AND BUTTER: In a medium metal bowl, combine the chocolates and butter. Create a makeshift double boiler by filling a pot with 1 inch of water (make sure the pot will comfortably hold the medium bowl without letting the bottom of the bowl touch the water). Bring the water to a simmer, reduce the heat, and set the bowl of chocolate and butter on the pot. Stir with a heat-resistant spatula from time to time until completely melted. Turn off the heat and carefully remove the bowl from the pot (use oven mitts or folded kitchen towels).

3. MAKE THE BATTER: In the bowl of an electric mixer fitted with the whisk attachment, beat the egg on high speed for about 1 minute. Add the sugar and vanilla and beat on high until the mixture thickens and becomes a pale yellow color, 4 to 5 minutes, stopping once to scrape down the sides and bottom of the bowl. Using a rubber spatula, stir in the chocolate mixture. Sift the flour, baking powder, and cocoa into the bowl, then add the salt. Slowly add the flour mixture to the chocolate and stir only until combined.

4. BAKE THE COOKIES: Drop scant tablespoons of the batter onto the baking sheets, leaving about 1½ inches between each to allow for spreading. You should have about nine mounds on each pan (eighteen total). Bake for 8 minutes, just until the tops of the cookies no longer look raw. Leave them on the pan for 10 minutes; they will be very soft straight out of the oven but will firm up quickly. After 10 minutes, transfer to a wire rack to cool completely. Use for ice cream sandwiches or serve as is. Store in an airtight container for up to 3 days.

prep time: 25 to 30 minutes
(plus at least 3 hours to chill the
caramel and 6 hours to chill the
assembled pudding)
cook time: 6 to 8 minutes
yield: 8 to 10 servings

LAYERED "BANOFFEE" BANANA PUDDING ICEBOX CAKE

Once in a while, my mom and I walk to Billy's Bakery in Manhattan and get some of their tasty banana icebox cake. It's a classic American dessert that is super fun to assemble and really impressive when you unmold and eat it. I've always wanted to make a version of this at home, and I came up with this recipe made of wafer cookies, homemade caramel sauce, and whipped cream that we make together—Mom usually makes the caramel while I make the whipped cream. Caramel can be tricky and even a little dangerous since the sugar is molten-hot; it's best to get a kitchen buddy or parent involved here. A few notes about sugar caramel: the pans and utensils have to be super clean because sugar gets grumpy and clumps up otherwise. Be patient. Be careful. Although the sugar may look pretty, it is very hot. You could also sub in a store-bought caramel sauce.

CARAMEL SAUCE

1 cup **granulated sugar**

1 cup **heavy cream**

1 tablespoon **vanilla extract**

1 teaspoon **kosher salt**

1 tablespoon **cornstarch**

WHIPPED CREAM

1 cup cold **heavy cream**

1 tablespoon **granulated sugar**

1. MAKE THE CARAMEL SAUCE: In a small saucepan over medium heat, combine 3 tablespoons water with the granulated sugar. Gently swirl the pan to moisten any dry sugar. (Try not to get any sugar granules on the sides of the pan, as they can scorch and burn while the caramel is cooking.) Leave the pan over medium heat, not stirring, until a caramel color begins to develop in spots, about 6 minutes. Continue to cook, swirling occasionally (don't stir), until the caramel is a deep amber color, an additional 1 to 2 minutes. Remove the pan from the heat and immediately whisk in the cream, vanilla, and salt. Return to the heat and allow to cook for an additional 30 seconds. Transfer to a heat-resistant container, cool completely, and refrigerate until thickened, 3 to 4 hours.

2. WHIP THE CREAM: In the bowl of an electric mixer fitted with the whisk attachment, whip the cream on medium-high speed until it becomes fluffy and you can see traces of the whisk in the cream. Beat in the granulated sugar.

(recipe and ingredients continue)

BANANA PUDDING

1 tablespoon **dark brown sugar**

1 (11-ounce) box **vanilla wafer cookies**

4 large ripe **bananas** (but not so ripe that they can't hold their shape after peeling)

3. MAKE THE FILLING: Scoop ¼ cup of the chilled caramel sauce into a small bowl and set aside. Add the remaining caramel sauce and the cornstarch to the whipped cream and fold until no streaks remain. Peel 3 bananas and slice into ¼-inch-thick rounds.

4. ASSEMBLE THE PUDDING: Line the insides of a 2½-quart bowl with plastic wrap. Put 1 tablespoon of the brown sugar into a little dish or bowl and set aside. Line the inside of the prepared bowl with the wafers, flat side up. Continue placing wafers in the bowl, up and around the sides, until you have an outer layer covering the entire inside of the bowl.

5. Spoon one-third of the whipped cream mixture into the center of the wafer-lined bowl. Top with a layer of sliced bananas and sprinkle the bananas with a pinch of brown sugar. Place the bowl in the freezer for 15 minutes to allow this layer to chill. Place another layer of wafers into the bowl, this time drizzling with a teaspoon of the reserved caramel sauce. Repeat the process twice more, dividing the remaining whipped cream mixture, more bananas, and brown sugar between the two layers. Finish by placing a layer of wafers along the top of the bowl for structure (this forms the bottom of the cake)—flat side up.

6. REFRIGERATE: Fold the plastic wrap over the final layer of the wafers and refrigerate the pudding for at least 6 hours or, ideally, overnight, along with the remaining caramel sauce.

7. SERVE: To unmold, peel the plastic wrap away from the bottom of the cake, set a plate on top, and, holding the plate with both hands, flip the plate and bowl over so the plate is on the bottom and the bowl is inverted on top. Lift off the bowl and peel away the plastic wrap. Peel and slice the reserved banana into rounds. Decorate the pudding with the banana slices and the reserved caramel sauce over top.

prep time: 20 minutes (plus at least 30 minutes for chilling the topping)
cook time: 25 to 35 minutes
yield: 4 to 6 servings

STRAWBERRY SKILLET CRISP

My grandma was famous for her apple and blueberry crisps and crumbles. I wanted to make a variation inspired by her and decided to use strawberries enhanced with lemon and raspberry. It's so good. It tastes like the best strawberry *ever* (even if you get out-of-season strawberries—shhhh, don't tell my mom). I strongly suggest you serve it warm with vanilla ice cream—and eat leftovers spooned over yogurt, toast, or pancakes for breakfast.

CRISP TOPPING

½ cup **rolled oats**

¼ cup **all-purpose flour**

¼ cup packed **dark brown sugar**

1 teaspoon ground **cinnamon**

1 teaspoon **kosher salt**

½ stick (4 tablespoons) **unsalted butter**, cubed and chilled

STRAWBERRY FILLING

2 tablespoons **extra-virgin olive oil**

8 cups (2 pounds) medium **strawberries**, hulled and quartered

½ cup **raspberry jam**

Zest and juice of 1 large **lemon**

½ cup **granulated sugar**

1 tablespoon **cornstarch**

1. MAKE THE TOPPING: In a medium bowl, combine the oats, flour, brown sugar, cinnamon, and salt. Work the butter in with your fingers until the mixture resembles coarse peas; it should be clumpy. Spread the mixture out on a baking sheet and place in the freezer for at least 30 minutes and up to 6 hours.

2. MAKE THE FILLING: In an 8-inch heavy-bottomed oven-safe sauté pan, heat 1 tablespoon of the olive oil over medium heat. When the oil begins to smoke lightly, remove the pan from the heat and add half the strawberries. Return the pan to the heat, increase to high, and cook for 1 minute, just to allow some of the water to escape. Transfer the berries to a colander set inside a large bowl so the juices separate from the fruit, then return the pan to the heat. Repeat with the remaining 1 tablespoon olive oil and the remaining strawberries.

3. THICKEN: Add the jam, lemon zest, and granulated sugar to the same pan. Pour the liquid that escaped from the strawberries into the pan as well. In a small bowl, whisk together the lemon juice and cornstarch until smooth and pour over the jam mixture. While whisking, bring the mix to a simmer over medium heat and reduce until thick and smooth, 1 to 2 minutes. Remove the colander and combine all the liquid with the berries in the bowl and stir to combine.

4. Preheat the oven to 375°F.

5. ASSEMBLE AND BAKE: Return the berries and all the liquid to the pan. Arrange all the crisp topping in an even layer over the fruit and place the pan on a baking sheet so that nothing falls or burns on the oven floor. Bake for 20 to 25 minutes or until the top browns and the fruit bubbles. Remove from the oven and cool for at least 30 minutes before serving.

prep time: 10 minutes
cook time: 5 to 10 minutes
yield: 4 servings

EGGLESS CHOCOLATE MOUSSE

This started as a Mom recipe but is something easy and homemade that I now like to make, too. Like my mom, I love chocolate mousse as a stand-alone dessert, but this is also a really easy way to make a filling to go between the layers of a cake, to top a birthday cake (page 222) or cupcakes (page 220), or as part of a parfait with mixed fruits and crushed-up cookies for some serious dessert drama. One little trick I have learned is that not completely mixing ingredients can sometimes make food more tasty. The honey, chocolate, and cream, almost but not completely combined, mean that one bite may have more chocolate and another more honey . . . that variety in flavors when eating is exciting. This mousse is based on a ganache recipe, which is just melted chocolate mixed with cream that has whipped cream folded into it. It's luscious and easy! Be warned, this mousse isn't super sweet, so you can top with a sprinkle of sugar for texture or a squeeze of honey for an almost caramel flavor.

2 cups **heavy cream**

2 tablespoons **honey**

1½ cups **semisweet chocolate**, finely chopped

1. MAKE THE GANACHE: In a small saucepan, heat 1 cup of the cream and 1 tablespoon of the honey over medium heat. Add the chocolate to a small bowl that fits over the pot with the cream and set it on top. (You're essentially using the pot of cream as the bottom of the double boiler and melting the chocolate on top!) Stir occasionally with a silicone spatula until the chocolate is melted. Transfer the cream to a large bowl and allow both the chocolate and cream to cool slightly, separately. When both are still somewhat warm (after about 5 minutes), add the chocolate to the cream and whisk together to combine.

2. WHIP THE CREAM: In the bowl of an electric mixer fitted with the whisk attachment, whip the remaining 1 cup cream on medium-low speed until it becomes fluffy and you can see traces of the whisk in the cream. Drizzle the remaining 1 tablespoon honey over the whipped cream but do not mix in.

3. ASSEMBLE: Using a rubber spatula, gently fold half the whipped cream into the chocolate-cream mixture (still slightly warm) until incorporated. Fill small bowls or ramekins with the mousse and chill 1 hour (or up to 6 hours) before serving dolloped with the remaining whipped cream.

prep time: 15 minutes
cook time: 25 to 30 minutes
yield: 6 to 8 servings

BAKED APPLES
with brown sugar + orange liqueur

As far as apple varieties go, nothing is more reliable than a tart, sturdy Granny Smith, but if you come across Rome, Macoun, or Cameo apples, you can use those, too, because they are juicy, firm, and distinctive in flavor. (My grandma's favorite was a Braeburn apple.) If you don't want to add the orange liqueur, simply sub in the juice of a large orange.

1 tablespoon **unsalted butter**, at room temperature

6 medium-firm **apples**, cored

Zest and juice of 1 large **lemon**

1 cup **apple cider**

¼ cup **Grand Marnier** or **Triple Sec** (or fresh orange juice)

1 cup packed **dark brown sugar**

½ teaspoon **kosher salt**

2 teaspoons ground **cinnamon**

1 teaspoon ground **ginger**

¼ teaspoon **nutmeg** (preferably freshly grated)

Vanilla ice cream, frozen yogurt, or **lemony sorbet**, for serving

1. Preheat the oven to 375°F.

2. GET READY: Grease the bottom and sides of a round oven-safe baking dish (about 2 quarts) with the butter. Arrange the apples in the dish (preferably in a circle if your baking dish can accommodate that). In a medium bowl, whisk together the lemon zest and juice, apple cider, Grand Marnier, brown sugar, salt, cinnamon, ginger, and nutmeg. Pour the mixture over the apples and place the baking dish in the center of the oven.

3. BAKE THE APPLES: Bake until the apples are tender in the center when pierced with the tip of a knife but not falling apart, 25 to 30 minutes. About halfway through the cooking process, take the dish out of the oven and use a large metal spoon to baste the apples with the juices that have built up in the bottom of the pan. Return the pan to the oven to finish cooking.

4. FINISH: Once the apples are tender, remove them from the oven. Carefully use a metal spatula or a large spoon to hold the apples in place while you pour the liquid from the baking dish into a small saucepan. Place the pan over medium heat and cook until syrupy, 2 to 3 minutes. Pour the sauce back over the apples.

5. SERVE: Serve as is or with vanilla ice cream, frozen yogurt, or even a lemony sorbet. Store any leftovers covered in plastic wrap in the refrigerator for up to 3 days.

prep time: 15 to 20 minutes
(plus 30 minutes to set)
cook time: 3 to 5 minutes
yield: 4 servings
equipment: 4 sturdy wooden sticks

CANDY APPLES

This recipe was born from trips to Disneyland and eating candy apples from the candy shop on Main Street USA. Ava and I both loved them so much that we had to create a homemade version to enjoy in between trips to Disney. These apples double as a confection and as aromatherapy for the kitchen. The aroma also takes us to that fall moment of the year when caramel and apples show up everywhere when pumpkin spice would be too . . . expected. After dipping, I like to roll them in coconut and nuts to make them *extra*. I use Granny Smith because they're tart—which is excellent against the sweet candy coating. Soft Rome, Braeburn, and Fuji apples all make me happy, too.

2 cups **sugar**

4 medium-firm **apples** (like Granny Smith)

Nonstick cooking spray

½ cup chopped **pecans**

½ cup **sweetened shredded coconut**

1. MAKE THE SUGAR COATING: In a dry medium pot, spread the sugar evenly. Over low heat, melt the sugar until it dissolves and becomes golden, 3 to 5 minutes (see Mom Tip!). Meanwhile, wash and thoroughly dry each apple. Turn off the heat. The caramel only needs to cool for a few minutes before you dip in the apples.

2. CANDY THE APPLES: Line a baking sheet with parchment paper and lightly coat with cooking spray. Place the pecans and the coconut on separate plates and set aside. Put each apple on an individual stick, then dip and gently swirl each apple in the caramel so they're coated. Turn the apples onto the prepared baking sheet, sticks pointing up. Roll the ends in either pecans or coconut before the sugar cools. (If the sugar hardens while dipping, warm it over low heat until it loosens.)

3. SERVE: Allow the apples to harden for at least 30 minutes and up to 4 hours before serving. Store at room temperature (the refrigerator will make the sugar weepy and soggy), covered in plastic wrap.

Mom Tip

Boiling sugar to make a simple caramel is one of the simplest—and hardest!—things to do. Be careful! Use a heavy-bottomed pot and make sure it's clean because impurities can mix with the sugar and make it clumpy. Don't use any utensils to stir the sugar either. Just swirl it gently and move the pot around as the sugar melts and browns.

photographs on pages 208–209

prep time: 25 minutes (plus at least 4 hours for chilling the pie)
cook time: 10 to 12 minutes
yield: 8 to 10 servings

FROZEN PEANUT BUTTER PIE

We definitely have lots of food traditions in my house. Every Thanksgiving, I make the same few pies that my mother (Ava's grandmother) used to bake—including classic pecan, sour cream-pumpkin, and cranberry-apple, as well as Italian cookies. One year, Ava came into the kitchen holding a *Martha Stewart Living* magazine open to the recipe for this pie. "Mom," she announced, "we need a new pie type in our family, and I think this is the one." Ava made the pie, tweaking the recipe here and there—adding chocolate chips for texture, adjusting the amounts of sugar, and changing the base of the crust to graham cracker. "Don't tell Martha we changed around her pie so much!" she giggled as she popped it into the freezer. I watched as people passed over classic pecan and pumpkin pies in favor of this new pie tradition. Note that using a premade graham cracker crust will save on some time and work.

GRAHAM CRACKER CRUST

(or use store-bought)

½ stick (4 tablespoons) **unsalted butter**, melted, plus extra at room temperature for greasing

1½ cups finely ground **graham cracker crumbs** (from about 10 whole graham crackers; a food processor makes swift work of this)

¼ cup **granulated sugar**

½ teaspoon ground **cinnamon**

PIE

8 ounces (1 cup) **full-fat cream cheese**, at room temperature (not whipped cream cheese)

¾ cup **confectioners' sugar**

1½ teaspoons **kosher salt**

1½ cups **smooth peanut butter**

2 teaspoons **vanilla extract**

1 teaspoon **blackstrap molasses**

2 cups **heavy cream**

1½ cups **semisweet chocolate chips**

(recipe continues)

1. Preheat the oven to 350°F.

2. GET READY: Grease the bottom and sides of a 9-inch pie dish with the butter and set aside.

3. MAKE THE CRUST: In a medium bowl, combine the graham cracker crumbs, granulated sugar, cinnamon, and melted butter. The texture should resemble wet sand. Transfer the mixture to the greased pie plate and use the bottom of a glass or a measuring cup to press the crust into an even layer in the bottom and up the sides of the pie plate. Place the pan in the oven and bake until the crust firms up and browns lightly, 10 to 12 minutes. Remove the pan from the oven and set aside to cool.

4. START THE FILLING: In the bowl of an electric mixer fitted with the paddle attachment, beat the cream cheese, confectioners' sugar, and salt on medium-high speed until fluffy, 2 to 3 minutes. Remove the bowl from the mixer and use a rubber spatula to fold in the peanut butter, vanilla, and molasses.

5. WHIP THE CREAM: In a clean bowl of the electric mixer, fitted with the whisk attachment, whip the cream on medium-low speed to soft peaks, until it becomes fluffy and you can see traces of the whisk in the cream.

6. FINISH: Using a rubber spatula, gently fold half the whipped cream into the peanut butter mixture and then fold in the rest. Spoon the filling into the fully cooled crust and place the pie plate in the freezer for at least 4 hours and up to 12 hours.

7. SERVE: Remove the pie from the freezer and top with the chocolate chips. Serve the pie in wedges. You can make this pie a day ahead, but allow it to stand for 15 to 20 minutes at room temperature to soften slightly before serving. Store any leftovers covered in plastic wrap in the freezer for up to 2 weeks.

CHOCOLATE CHIPS

PAN

PEANUT BUTTER FILLING

prep time: 40 minutes (plus 15 to 20 minutes for freezing the butter and 1 hour to cool the pie)
cook time: 35 to 45 minutes
yield: 8 to 10 servings

NOT GRANDMA'S BLUEBERRY PIE

When I was a kid (as Ava likes to say, "one thousand years ago"), I can't tell you how much I longed for the Fourth of July to roll around so my mom would bake a blueberry pie. Her filling was a little loose because she refused to add any cornstarch to thicken it—so the pie turned into a juicy, jammy blueberry soup. Heaven. The pie we are making here has much more structure because it truly is prettier to serve it that way. How best to eat this pie? My mother would pour straight chilled heavy cream over her slice and eat the spoonfuls of blueberry-laced cream with such joy. As is true with a lot of these recipes, you can control the difficulty level and make the crust in advance or simply use a store-bought one and make the filling. Your call.

DOUGH

2½ sticks **unsalted butter**, plus extra at room temperature for greasing

3 cups **all-purpose flour**, plus extra for rolling

1 tablespoon **sugar**

1 teaspoon **kosher salt**

½ teaspoon ground **cinnamon**

6 to 8 tablespoons **ice water**

1. GET READY: Pop the sticks of butter into your freezer for 15 to 20 minutes to get them extra chilled. Grease a 9-inch pie dish with the soft butter.

2. MAKE THE DOUGH: In the bowl of a food processor, pulse the flour, sugar, salt, and cinnamon together to blend. Using the largest-hole side of a box grater (or the grater attachment on a food processor), grate the butter. Add the butter to the dry ingredients and pulse 12 to 15 times until the mixture resembles coarse peas. (Do not overmix or the dough will be tough.) Add 6 tablespoons of the ice water through the feed tube and pulse until the dough comes together into a loose ball. If it's too dry (floury) and crumbly, add the remaining 2 tablespoons of water. Remove the blade from the food processor and set aside, then gather the dough and turn it out onto a floured surface. Press the dough together with your fingers so it feels smooth.

3. Preheat the oven to 375°F.

4. ROLL OUT THE DOUGH: Cut the dough in half, cover one of the halves in plastic wrap, and refrigerate. Flour the top of the remaining dough half and use a rolling pin to roll it into an 11- to 12-inch round, reflouring on top and beneath the dough as needed to prevent sticking. (If at any time the dough becomes sticky or soft, transfer it to a parchment-lined pan and refrigerate it until firm.)

FILLING

5 cups fresh **blueberries**

¾ cup **sugar**

5 tablespoons **cornstarch**

1 tablespoon each zest and juice from 1 medium **lemon**

2 tablespoons **light corn syrup**

½ teaspoon ground **cinnamon**

½ teaspoon **kosher salt**

8 ounces (about 1 cup) good-quality **blueberry jam** (we like Bonne Maman)

EGG WASH

1 large **egg yolk**

1 tablespoon **whole milk**

Vanilla ice cream, whipped cream, or a splash of **heavy cream**, for serving

Roll the dough around the rolling pin and unroll it over the greased pie dish. Press the dough gently into the bottom and up the sides of the pie dish—ideally, there should be about 1 inch of excess dough hanging over the sides. Pinch the dough up to create a crimped top edge. Place a sheet of parchment paper gently over the crust and fill it with pie weights or dried beans. Bake for 6 to 8 minutes or only until the edges are very lightly browned. Remove the pie dish from the oven and carefully lift out the parchment with the beans; set the bottom crust aside to cool.

5. MAKE THE FILLING: In a large bowl, use a large metal spoon to combine the blueberries, sugar, cornstarch, lemon zest and juice, corn syrup, cinnamon, and salt. Mix to blend. Stir in the jam.

6. ASSEMBLE: Fill the par-baked bottom crust with the filling. Remove the reserved half of dough from the refrigerator, unwrap it, and set it on a floured surface. Flour the top and roll it out the same as you did for the bottom crust. Roll the dough up onto the rolling pin and unroll over the top of the pie. Pinch the top to the bottom to make sure the edges are fluted and sealed shut all the way around. Use a pastry cutter or small knife to cut a 2-inch-long X in the center of the top. Fold back the four pieces of the dough made by the X, so it looks like the open pages of a book.

7. MAKE THE EGG WASH: In a small bowl, whisk the egg yolk with the milk until smooth. Use a pastry brush to brush the top crust, coating it completely. (This will give your crust a more golden look and a slightly richer taste.)

8. BAKE: Bake the pie for 35 to 40 minutes or until the top is golden brown. Remove the pan from the oven. Cool for at least 1 hour and, ideally, up to 4 hours to allow the filling to set. Cut into slices and serve with vanilla ice cream, whipped cream, or a splash of heavy cream. If there is any leftover pie, cover it in plastic wrap and refrigerate for up to 4 days.

photographs on pages 216–219

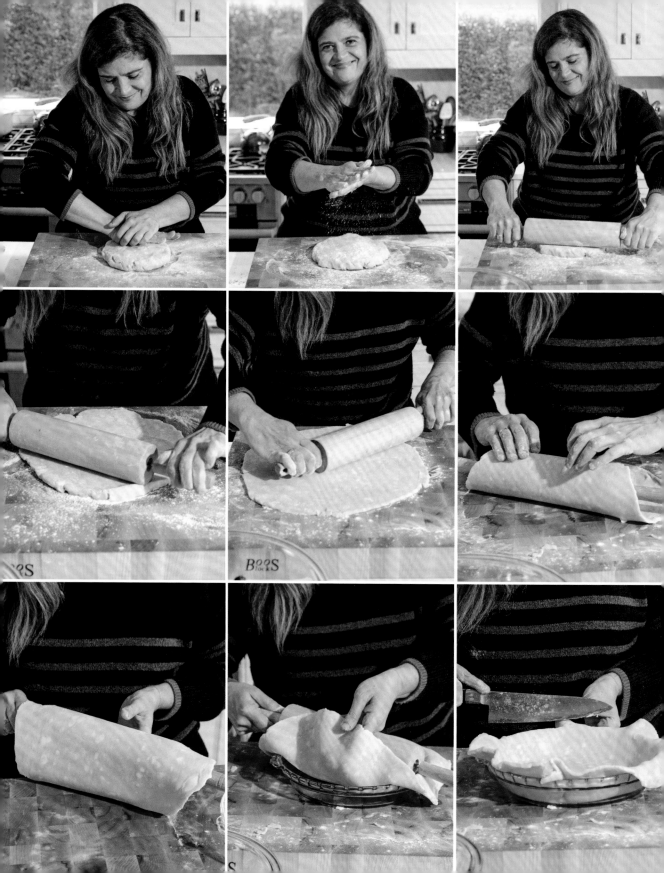

BLACK + WHITE CUPCAKES

prep time: 25 minutes (plus cooling)
cook time: 12 minutes
yield: 12 cupcakes

This is a serious cupcake batter that can go head-to-head with any local bakery's, and YOU are going to make it yourself! The result is a really moist and homemade cupcake with *two* kinds of chocolate. These cupcakes have so much flavor and richness without being super heavy—they're like a classic black-and-white cookie with the "white" being the white chocolate cupcake part and the "black" being the glaze you dunk them in. White chocolate is very rich and can be temperamental, so melt it gently and at the last minute before adding it to the batter. Chopping the chocolate into smaller pieces makes it easier to melt, too. You want the white chocolate warm and melted but neither hot nor completely cooled when you add it to your batter (see? temperamental). You can also use a cake mix for the cupcakes and simply make the glaze from this recipe to top them. Or you can just make the cupcakes from this recipe and buy a frosting or glaze. You decide how much of this you want to take on!

CUPCAKES

Nonstick cooking spray

2 large **eggs**, separated

1 stick (8 tablespoons) **unsalted butter**, at room temperature

⅔ cup **sugar**

1½ cups **all-purpose flour**

1 teaspoon **kosher salt**

1 teaspoon **baking powder**

½ teaspoon **baking soda**

½ cup **whole milk**

½ cup (4 ounces) **white chocolate**, coarsely chopped (not white chocolate chips)

1 tablespoon **vanilla extract**

½ cup **sour cream**, at room temperature

1. Preheat the oven to 325°F. Spray a 12-cup cupcake tin with nonstick spray and add a double layer of cupcake papers to each cup. Line a baking sheet with parchment paper and set a cooling rack on top.

2. WHIP THE EGG WHITES: In the bowl of an electric mixer fitted with the whisk attachment, whip the egg whites on high speed until stiff peaks form, about 3 minutes. Carefully transfer the egg whites to another bowl and wash the mixer bowl.

3. MAKE THE BATTER: In the clean bowl of the electric mixer fitted with the paddle attachment, beat the butter and sugar on medium speed until light and fluffy, 3 to 5 minutes. Meanwhile, mix together the flour, salt, baking powder, and baking soda in a medium bowl and set aside.

4. Add the egg yolks, one by one, to the butter-sugar mixture, beating on medium speed until each is fully incorporated.

5. In a small saucepan, warm the milk gently over medium-low heat and add the white chocolate and vanilla. Melt, stirring gently, until the white chocolate melts into the milk. Do not simmer or boil. This is a low-key melting chocolate moment! Transfer the milk mixture to a medium bowl and gently whisk in the sour cream. With the mixer on low, pour the white chocolate mixture into the butter-sugar-egg mixture in a steady stream. Mix until combined and scrape

GLAZE

4 ounces
dark chocolate (70%),
coarsely chopped
(about ½ cup)

¼ cup **heavy cream**

1 tablespoon **light corn syrup**

down the sides of the bowl with a spatula. Add the flour mixture, a spoonful at a time, folding after each, until the batter just comes together. Fold the reserved egg whites into the batter, again just until combined. Add about ½ cup batter to each cupcake cup, filling to the top.

6. BAKE: Lightly tap the pan a few times on a flat surface to level the batter and eliminate air pockets, then bake for 12 minutes. Rotate the pan and bake for an additional 4 minutes or until the edges start to turn golden brown and a cake tester inserted into the center of a cupcake emerges clean. Remove the pan from the oven and allow the cupcakes to cool on the rack for 5 minutes. Then carefully remove the cupcakes from the pan so the heat doesn't dry them out. Cool completely.

7. MAKE THE GLAZE: In a small heat-resistant bowl, melt the dark chocolate over a pot of simmering water, making sure the bottom of the bowl doesn't touch the simmering water (this is a double boiler). In a small saucepan, gently warm the cream over low heat. Stir in the corn syrup. When the chocolate has melted, remove the bowl from the heat and stir the chocolate into the cream mixture.

8. FINISH: The cupcakes should be completely cooled when you glaze them. Dip the top of each cupcake in the glaze, then place them on a flat surface to allow the glaze to set up. Eat right away or leave at room temperature (loosely covered) for up to 3 days.

VANILLA BIRTHDAY CAKE
with chocolate ganache

prep time: 30 minutes
(plus cooling and chilling)
cook time: 30 to 35 minutes
yield: 1 (9-inch) two-layer
cake; 12 to 14 servings

This is a signature Mom recipe and is her favorite cake to make—it's the one we always make to celebrate our birthdays. I'm not a cake person at all . . . but when I crave a scratch-made cake, this is the one I love the most. It's fluffy, light, and has tons of flavor. The egg whites and the milk add to its snow-white color, and with the dark chocolate ganache on top, it's a dynamite combo. One note: The ingredients for this cake MUST be at room temperature for the batter to work. Also, you'll need two 9-inch cake pans to make it.

CAKE

2½ sticks (20 tablespoons) **unsalted butter**, at room temperature, plus extra for greasing the pans

2¼ cups **sugar**

1½ cups **whole milk**, at room temperature

1 tablespoon plus 2 teaspoons **vanilla extract**

4½ cups **cake flour**

2 tablespoons **baking powder**

1 teaspoon **kosher salt**

7 large **egg whites**, at room temperature

½ teaspoon **cream of tartar**

GANACHE

1 cup **heavy cream**

2 cups finely chopped **semisweet chocolate**

Rainbow sprinkles (optional)

1. Preheat the oven to 350°F. Grease 2 (9-inch) cake pans with softened butter.

2. START THE BATTER: In the bowl of an electric mixer fitted with the paddle attachment, cream the butter and sugar on medium speed until fluffy, 6 to 8 minutes. (Do not rush this step. The sugar is softening and fluffing the butter, and this is part of what gives a great cake its great texture. Be patient—you'll be rewarded.) Once it's adequately fluffy, decrease the mixer speed to low and add the milk and vanilla in a steady but very slow, small stream, allowing it to integrate fully before adding more. Adding the milk should take at least 3 to 4 minutes with the mixer running the whole time on low speed. Turn off the mixer.

3. FINISH THE BATTER: To a fine-mesh sieve, add the flour, baking powder, and salt and sift into the batter, using a rubber spatula to fold until combined—the batter shouldn't have any pockets of unmixed flour. Do not overmix; overmixing makes for a tough, chewy cake. Transfer the batter to a large bowl and wash clean the mixer bowl, leaving no trace of fat behind (this would prevent the egg whites from whipping up nicely, which they must do in the next step).

4. WHIP AND ADD THE EGG WHITES: In the super-clean bowl of the electric mixer fitted with the whisk attachment, whip the egg whites and cream of tartar on medium speed until soft peaks form, 2 to 3 minutes. Using a rubber spatula, gently fold the whites into the batter. Divide the batter between the prepared cake pans, smoothing out the tops and taking care to treat the batter gently so it doesn't deflate.

(recipe continues)

5. BAKE: Place the cake pans side by side on the center oven rack and bake for 25 to 30 minutes, until a small knife or toothpick inserted into the center of the cake comes out clean. Remove the pans from the oven and let the cakes cool in the pans for about 15 minutes. Run a paring knife around the edges to ensure they aren't sticking and unmold the cakes onto a wire rack to cool completely.

6. MAKE THE GANACHE: In a small saucepan, heat the cream over medium heat. In a small bowl that fits over the pot with the cream, add the chocolate (make sure the bottom of the bowl doesn't touch the cream). Reduce the heat to medium-low and use the pot of cream as the bottom of the double boiler to melt the chocolate, stirring occasionally until completely melted. Remove the bowl from the saucepan and set aside. Pour the cream from the saucepan into a bowl and set aside to cool slightly. While the cream is still somewhat warm, whisk the cream into the melted chocolate and set aside for at least 15 minutes and up to 30 minutes before frosting the cake.

7. ASSEMBLE: Place the bottom layer of the cake, top facing down, on a cake plate and spread a thin layer of the ganache over top. Add the second layer squarely on top and frost the top and sides of the cake with the remaining ganache. Decorate with rainbow sprinkles, if desired. Let the frosted cake set for at least 1 hour and up to 8 hours before serving. You can loosely wrap the cake and refrigerate it for up to 3 days. Let it come back to room temperature before serving.

CHOPPED CHOCOLATE

STEAM

CREAM

BONUS RECIPE!

A family that eats treats
and desserts together stays
together, so . . .

prep time: 15 minutes
(plus cooling)
cook time: 15 to 20 minutes
yield: 26 to 28 biscuits

LEON'S DOG BISCUITS

Almost full credit has to go to the resident food stylist on this book project, Melanie Stuparyk, for hatching this actual recipe with so much love. I can only take real credit for the peanut butter topping in the paw print. Leon is the most special addition to our family, and Melanie is a dog mom, too. We wanted a tasty biscuit, one you might be *tempted* to eat yourself but that has lots of healthy ingredients for a dog, namely, peanut butter and oats. During the photo shoot, we decided to create a special treat for Leon, and I can say that he is OBSESSED with these. When we gave him a couple to try out, he devoured them! That told us all we needed to know. So, when you are making holiday cookies or thinking of a fun homemade gift for friends or family members who have dogs, this is a great way to flex. Note: If your dog is small, roll out the dough and cut it into small bite-size squares, using a pizza cutter or a knife. Adjust the baking time as needed—you want to bake them until they are brown and dry. To save time, you can also just coat the biscuits lightly with peanut butter and forgo the little dots for paw prints.

BISCUIT DOUGH

1 cup **whole-wheat flour**

1 cup **rolled oats**

1 large ripe **banana**, mashed

2 tablespoons **smooth natural peanut butter**

1 to 2 tablespoons **chicken broth** or **water**

All-purpose flour

PAW FROSTING

4 to 5 tablespoons **smooth natural peanut butter**

½ teaspoon ground **cinnamon**

1. Preheat the oven to 350°F. Line a baking sheet with parchment paper.

2. MAKE THE DOUGH: In a large bowl, use a large spoon to stir together the whole-wheat flour and oats and make a well in the center of the mix. Add the banana, peanut butter, and broth and stir to combine. Use your hands to fully mix the dough together. It should feel soft so you can roll it into individual balls. If the dough is sticking a lot or feels wet, mix in a little all-purpose flour. If the dough is dry, add another tablespoon of broth.

3. FORM THE BISCUITS: On a flat, lightly floured surface, roll out the dough to a ⅛-inch thickness and use a 2-inch round cutter to cut out rounds, rerolling the scraps as needed. Place the rounds on the prepared baking sheet with a little space between each. Using the end of a wooden spoon, press paw-shaped indents into the biscuits.

4. BAKE: Bake the biscuits for 15 to 20 minutes or until browned and dry. Remove the pan from the oven and cool for at least 30 minutes and up to 6 hours.

5. MAKE THE FROSTING: In a small bowl, use a whisk to combine the peanut butter and cinnamon. Once the biscuits are cool, use your fingertip to apply a light smear of peanut butter mixture into each indent of the paw mark. Store the biscuits at room temperature in a sealed cookie jar or in a resealable plastic bag for up to 4 days.

ACKNOWLEDGMENTS

To the people who live on with us forever:

Mom (Grandma)

Dad (Grandpa)

Uncle George

Aunt Aggie

And Aunt Betsy DiBenedetto

My eternal thanks to Bobby Flay for his patient and unwavering guidance. He also happens to make the best pork chop and sea urchin pasta on the planet and offers so much chef-like and friend comfort beyond words. Thanks for cooking for me in so many ways.

Thanks to Giada De Laurentiis for being a great friend. So supportive and worthy of my admiration. I always need brownie nibble time and honest talk with you.

Enormous thanks to Guy Fieri, who always champions me through various shows on Food Network. He always makes me feel like an important part of his great work. If you can fog a mirror . . .

Thanks to Sunny Anderson for so much love and honesty. Verzuz!

Thanks to Brian Lando. He is the reason I am on a few shows called *Chopped* and *Iron Chef* and *Alex Versus America*. I honestly owe so much of my career to his belief in me. A special thanks to Steve Kroopnick and John Bravakis from Triage Entertainment, too. You guys just love to follow me around with a camera and watch me cook great food and burn stuff, too. Thanks to Jesse Belodoff— you love the craft of cooking and I appreciate you for it.

The most important chef I ever worked for is Guy Savoy. He told this scrappy American girl it was okay to cook in his 3-star Michelin joint in Paris in 1992, and that experience made me the cook that I am, flaws and all. He was so generous and kind to me at a time when that wasn't the most obvious way to act. He simply believed in me, and I can't thank him enough for the vote of confidence. It made me want to become a chef.

Besides my daughter, my other great life achievement is Butter. A force of nature. We called it "Butter: We can't believe it's still open" for a few years there . . . and twenty-one years later: wow. It's mostly because we all want to be Alvaro Buchelly when we grow up. It wouldn't be Butter without chef Michael "Butter is an Italian restaurant" Jenkins, the incredible Jamaal "Edward 40hands" Dunlap, Antonio "à la Morales" Morales, pastry chef extraordinaire Kevin O'Brien, Miguel "Mango" Angel Cruz, Flaviano "Muscle Milk" Sosa, Jon "I have Nothing!" Boros, Max "Picasso" Castro, DJSergel "You're fired again" Ramirez, Wirt "I need to take a gin break and run a juice bar because I now have 10 children" Cook, Diane "Can I just gently punch you once, Michael?" Vista-Wayne, Lucas "I have a sniffle" Marino, and many others. I call you all colleagues, but you are also family.

Thanks to Lauren Basco, Tony Ramirez, and Tim Gunyon for caring so much about the restaurant.

To amazing purveyors and friends: Pat LaFrieda, Mark Pastore, and Louis Rozzo. Great meat and fish are the building blocks of a restaurant that endures, and it's a testament to your dedication to the craft.

Thanks to the farmers at the Union Square Greenmarket: Stokes Farms, Cherry Lane Farm, Eckerton Farms, and Keith's Farm.

Thanks to great Hamptons farmers: Marilee Foster, Pike Farms, Balsam Farms, Green Thumb Organic, Amber Waves, Quail Hill Farm, and Armin and Judy. Thanks to Carissa's the Bakery and Provisions Sag Harbor for inspiring me, too.

Endless thanks to my editor, Raquel Pelzel. Raquel really worked so hard to make sure this book had the authority and teaching notes of a chef mixed with the pure, true voice of a fifteen-year-old. The devil is always in the details, and Raquel always wants to get that right. Thanks to the Clarkson Potter staff who pitched in: Kim Tyner,

Terry Deal, and Merri Ann Morrell. Thanks to Stephanie Huntwork for the stunning and unique design of the book. Thanks to Brianne Sperber for great marketing and David Hawk and Natalie Yera for their publicity work.

Thanks to Ken Goodman for his amazing photos, love of all food, and a chilled negroni. You are incredible!

Thanks to photographers Alyssa Wodebek and Chris Sue-Chu from Suech and Beck for their playful vision of food. Thanks to Melanie Stuparyk and her passionate assistant, Jonah Snitman (who makes tasty ramen).

Thanks to Kate Fitzpatrick, Veronica Lee, and Lucia Vazquez for expert support, food styling, and recipe testing.

Thanks to Irika Slavin, Lauren Mueller, and Sierra Gray at Food Network for their amazing support and patience. Special thanks to Kathleen Finch for taking a chance on me more than once! Thanks to Betsy Ayala, Nick Briscoe, and Lynn Sadofsky for the vote of confidence!

Special thanks to Jon Steinlauf, Karen Grinthal, and Jon Sichel for their great friendship.

Thanks to Josh Bider, Jeff Googel, Strand Conover, and Jon Rosen at William Morris Endeavor.

Thanks to Lee Schrager for being a wonderful friend!

Thanks to Colleen Grapes for being the absolute best. Thanks to Billy Bar Chord, Randy Kolhoff, Peter Cook, Alba Jancou, Karen "Kiki" Mullane, MP Styles, Patti Jackson, Missy Robbins, Jeremy and Jarhn Blutstein, Katie Lee Biegel, Scott Conant, Antonia Lofaso, Mikey "Bagels," and fellow chefs everywhere.

Special thanks to Dave "D money" Mechlowicz for being an amazing friend.

Thanks to my dad, Brandon Clark, and my nan and pop, Madi and Alan Clark. Love to my Uncle Rory, too.

And lastly, thanks to Leon Duval le Chiffre, our Mini Aussie, for bringing great love and healing to Ava and me when we really needed it. Leon, you can chew my shoes anytime.

INDEX

Note: Page references in *italics* indicate photographs of completed recipes.

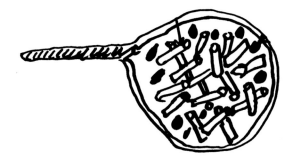